SHOWING THE STORY

SHOWING THE STORY

Creative Nonfiction by New Writers

Collected and Edited by Guy Allen
and the Life Rattle Collective

LIFE RATTLE PRESS TORONTO, CANADA

Showing the Story
Creative Nonfiction by New Writers

Published in Canada by Life Rattle Press, Toronto

2 3 4 5 6 7 8 9   21 20 19 18 17 16 15 14

Library and Archives Canada Cataloguing in Publication

Showing the story : creative nonfiction by new writers
/ collected and edited by Guy Allen and the Life Rattle Collective.
(New writers series)
Summary: A collection for short narrative nonfiction stories
written by new writers from the greater Toronto area.

ISBN 978-1-927023-63-1 (pbk.)

1. Creative nonfiction, Canadian (English)--Ontario--
Toronto.
I. Allen, Guy, 1947-, editor of compilation
II. Life Rattle Collective, editor of compilation
III. Series: Life Rattle new writers series

PS8257.T67S56 2014   C814'.60809713541   C2014-901080-X

Edited by: Guy Allen, John Dunford and Laurie Kallis
Cover Design by Laurie Kallis
Cover Illustration by Lena Spoke
Typeset by Laurie Kallis

Contents

Chapter 1: The Child

Chapter 2: School

Chapter 3: Family

Chapter 4: Relationships

Chapter 5: People

Chapter 6: Places

Chapter 7: Work

Chapter 8: The Interview

Preface

This collection contains sixty-eight short prose pieces by new writers for new writers. Although several of these authors have gone on to have work published and presented in public readings, none had substantial experience in prose before they developed these pieces as assignments. Almost none of the authors in this book had ever thought to call themselves writers.

We have put this collection together with an academic setting in mind, but the writing here—bold, entertaining, fresh—will engage readers who take pleasure in stories.

Like *No More Masterpieces*, the peer-model narrative collection that mapped the trail, *Showing the Story* reinforces my feeling that most of the expressive potential in our society remains unvoiced.

Given opportunity and support, many among us can create moving, sensitive, funny, shocking, sad, informative writing. No good reason exists why a select few should monopolize the pleasure, the power, and the release available through expression. The people who worked on this collection hope it will provoke others to take up their pens.

Guy Allen
University of Toronto
January, 2014

Chapter 1: The Child

Present a short, detailed account
of an experience you had as a child.

Guilt

Sunny Ahn

S o," Mom yells, "your little five-year-old brother is the one to
blame?"

"No," I murmur.

"I'm taking one of you upstairs. Who will it be?"

I stand silent. Sungho, my little brother, cries. Mom grabs
Sungho's wrist and drags him upstairs. I remain in the living room.

"I'm gonna teach you a lesson," Mom tells Sungho. His soft cries
turn into screams of fear.

I know Mom's weapon of choice—a long, blue, plastic Little
Tikes golf stick.

I cry for Sungho. I cry softly. I don't want Mom to return.

Bam! A door slams. Mom yells at Sungho. I run halfway up the
stairs to listen. I do not want to get caught in front of the bedroom
door.

Mom yells in Korean. Sungho screams.

"*Hyung* did!" he cries. Hyung means "older brother" in Korean.

"Well, Hyung said you did it. Give me your hand!"

I scrunch my face. I listen to the slaps on Sungho's tiny hands.
He screams loud. I'm a horrible brother, I think.

Jeehyun, my little sister, approaches me on the staircase.

"Poor Sungho," she says.

"Yeah," I say.

Jeehyun squeezes her eyes shut with every slap.

I cover my ears. We both keep our heads down.

Sungho screams louder. He sounds desperate. The slapping goes on and on. Mom knows I'm listening.

I grab Jeehyun's hand and rush down the stairs. I turn on the television. *SpongeBob SquarePants* plays. Tears run down Jeehyun's pink cheeks. The house goes quiet. Mom must be done.

The door opens. The hinges squeak. Mom walks slowly down the stairs and into the kitchen. She ignores us and sits at the kitchen table.

Silence.

I hide behind the wall and spy on Mom. She sits motionless. The sun shines on her face. She cries.

I run upstairs. Sungho lies on the bed. He sweats. Blankets, pillows and the plastic golf stick lie scattered on the floor. Closed curtains cover the windows.

"Hey, you okay?" I ask.

Silence.

I lie down next to Sungho. He puts his arms around me. I hug him.

"Hyung, I'm sorry," he says. Sungho is innocent. His apology hits me like a brick.

"Sorry for being a bad brother," I say. I hug him tighter.

Mom cries, Sungho cries, I cry.

Mom and I don't talk for a week. Sungho, I think, is a better brother than me.

I feel guilty.

I also feel glad I did not get beaten.

Sesame Street

Laurel Waterman

I don't want to stay in bed anymore, though I hear no cars on Duplex Avenue and the sky is just starting to lighten outside my bedroom window. I can't hear anything inside the house. I scramble my feet out from under the sheet and slide down from my pink canopy bed onto the shaggy green rug. I feel crumbs with my bare feet as I walk the two steps from my bed to the door. The hinges squeak as I pull the door open.

The narrow hall to Daddy's room seems long and dark. I see only shapes. The wooden railing guides my trip to the end. Daddy's breathing gets louder. He snorts at the end of each breath, pauses, then starts a new one. I stand in the doorway. He looks different without his glasses—like someone else's daddy.

He's alone, no lady friend beside him this morning. I tiptoe to the side of the bed.

"Daddy," I say, "can I go downstairs and watch *Sesame Street?*"

"Umhmm."

Silence.

"Daddy?" I poke his hairy ear.

"What does the clock say?"

I read the red numbers off the clock radio beside his bed.

"It says 6-4-7."

"When it says 7-0-0, it's time for *Sesame Street*," he mumbles. Usually he speaks slowly, in a loud, low voice. Now he whispers.

Hot air blows out of the metal vent on the floor beside his bed. I sit on the vent and make a tent over my knees with my faded pink nightgown, the one with a padded Raggedy Ann face on the front. I play with her red yarn braids and stare at the clock. I put a braid in my mouth and chew.

"Daddy, it changed to 6-4-8!"

"When it says 7-0-0 you can go downstairs and turn on the TV."

Daddy scratches his nose and rubs his eyes. He doesn't open them. His big nostrils stretch when he breathes in. I can see up his nose. I don't have nostril hair like he does. He has dents on his nose where his glasses usually sit. He looks better with his glasses on.

"Daddy, how much longer until 7-0-0?"

No answer.

I curl up and fold my arms and face into the nightgown tent. The heat puffs my nightgown out. The warm air feels nice blowing on my skin. I play with my toes.

"Daddy, how much longer?"

"About ten minutes." He yawns without moving.

I stare at his face and his long bushy eyebrows. A few silver, wiry ones reach halfway up his forehead. I want to touch his bald spot. It's soft.

The warm air stops and my puffed-out nightgown deflates. The heat seeps out. I get goosebumps.

"Daddy, you look better with your glasses on."

His eyes open halfway. He studies me for a second and smiles. "You're just used to seeing me with them on."

He flips the comforter back and sits on the edge of the bed. His feet look big at the bottom of his skinny, hairy ankles. A few strands of his grey hair stick straight out on the left side of his head.

He reaches to the nightstand, finds his glasses and puts them on.

"Okay, sweetheart." Daddy holds out his hand. I take it and he pulls me up. "Let's go downstairs."

I trail behind him down the hallway.

Daddy walks down the creaky stairs. "What do you think, pancakes or french toast for breakfast?"

I smile. "Blueberry pancakes."

"I think we can manage that."

I stop halfway and plop down on the middle stair and bum my way down the rest.

"Daddy?"

"Yes, sweetheart?"

"Is it time for *Sesame Street* yet?"

Behind the Cedars

Penny Verbruggen

I crouch, wait and watch from behind the prickly cedar bushes.
"Hey, Ver-brace-face, come out, come out, wherever you are!"

I play hide-and-seek with Janet and Debbi nearly every afternoon before Dad comes home from work. Mom cooks supper. I smell stinky brussels sprouts. I hate brussels sprouts. They give me a stomachache. Dad hates brussels sprouts, too, but he never talks back to Mom. Just once I want Dad to say, "No more brussels sprouts! We despise brussels sprouts."

I spy Janet's feet through the twiggy branches.

"You think she's near here, Janet?" asks Debbi.

"Yeah. She's too dumb to hide good. She always gets caught close to her house."

Debbi laughs. "She's such a baby," she sings in a mocking voice. "I can't stay out with you cuz my mommy doesn't want me to. I'm gonna get in trouble."

Debbi and Janet move away from the cedars. My right eye itches. I rub it with my Peter Pointer finger, careful not to disturb the spider web near my bare shoulder. Gross. Bits of brittle leaves, chunks of dirt and cigarette foil stick to the web. I look for the spider. The cedars hurt and poke at my eyes. Fine cat-like scratches cover my legs and arms. An ant crawls over my toenail. "Phew!" I blow at a leggy mosquito on my bent arm.

"Where'd she go-o-o?" Janet's voice drifts from behind my house. She scours my usual hiding places.

"She always has to go home at five or her mama gets mad. Let's wait for her."

"Ha! We'll get her when she comes out. I wonder where she is, though."

Debbi and Janet hang out with me in July and August. They live on my street, Canterbury Street, but they don't go to my school. "You go to a Cat-licker school," they tease.

"Yeah, well I wouldn't go to a Pot-licker school. Pot-licker, Pot-licker," I scream back. Nothing ever works. During the school year, we have other friends.

Tires roll over the stones in the driveway. Daddy's home! The blue Chevy slows past the cedars. I hear the big car door open and slam shut. "Hi Debbi, Debbi ding-a-ling. How ya doin'?" Dad teases. "And look. It's Jeepers-Creepers Janet. How's your mom feeling?"

"Fine, Mr. Verbruggen. She's okay. We're playing hide-and-seek. Can you go see if Penny's in the house? We can't find her, and we looked eeeeeeverywhere."

I imagine Janet flinging her arms wide for effect.

"Sure. But I don't think she'd leave your game. I'll look anyway."

The wooden screen door sticks. Dad grumbles something about fixing it. Debbi and Janet wait.

I have to pee.

The screen door opens again. "Girls, Penny's not here. But it's almost five. She'll be in for supper. See ya later, ladies."

"Bye, Mr. Verbruggen."

Debbi and Janet kick stones down the driveway. A couple skid up the sidewalk inches from the cedars. I breathe in a bug, and snort it out. The game drags on, my eye itches, and the girls cannot find me. Better to pee in the dirt than to lose my hiding spot.

"I don't like her anymore. Let's not talk to her when she comes out, okay, Deb?"

"Who's gonna play hide-and-seek with us then?"

"Okay. We'll just hang with her for the holidays."

Debbi and Janet look across Canterbury Street to their homes. I pray for nice grade sixers to move on to Canterbury Street. I pray that Debbi and Janet will just go inside and not catch me peeing.

I slide my pink shorts and flowered panties to the side to let out the pee. The elastic band pulls at my damp skin. A warm stream runs over my fingers and down into the dry dirt. A dark spot grows next to the left heel of my pink rubber flip-flop.

Debbi and Janet skip away.

"Penny, come out, come out, wherever you are! It's your supper-time!" Dad yells through the metal screen.

Debbi and Janet talk a safe distance from the cedars, no longer caring about hide-and-seek or me. Bent like a troll, I force the dry cedar branches aside and tumble out into the five o'clock sunlight. I straighten, wipe my dirt-covered hands on my bloodied legs, and pull on the elastic of my cotton shorts. What if Mom finds out? I hope to God my shorts are still pink and clean. I rub the corner of my eye with a dirty thumb.

"Hi, Daddy!" I run into the house and hug Dad around the waist. His belt buckle feels cool against my skin. His nicotine-stained fingers pull cedar pieces from my hair.

"Hi, baby girl. Wow. Look at you. That was some hiding place. Let's get you cleaned up before Mom sees the mess."

I let go of Dad. He looks down into my eyes. "Holy smokes! Where did you get that stye? Have you been peein' in the bushes?" he asks. "You know that old rhyme?"

12

Dad begins singing a song about peeing in the bush and a stye in the eye.

Shame rips through my body. Shock paralyzes me.

Dad blinks as I weep.

"I promise. I'll never do it again, Daddy. I promise. Please don't tell Mom. Please."

Cow Plops

Evangeline Torres Sled

"N anay, did I really come out of a cow's butt?" I ask Mom.
"Yeah, you did Vangie!" Ate answers first.

My sister's older than me so I have to call her "Ate" out of respect—and not her nickname Acon or her real name Maricon.

"Acon, stop that!" Nanay squeaks.

I close our family album. I don't look like Ate. Her face is white
and fat like Nanay's.

"But, am I adopted then?"

"Why would you say that?"

"'Cause Nanay, how come you don't have any baby pictures of
me?"

"'Cause you were picked out of cow shit." Ate giggles and pinches
her nose. "Why do you think you're so dark and we're so light?"

"Acon!" Mom scolds Ate. "Vangie, look at your father. You're as
dark as Tatay and have his fat lips. No way you're adopted. Besides, I
told you already, we lost your baby photos at the airport."

"They didn't lose mine," Ate says.

I look like Tatay. Maybe I came out of him.

Ate and I sit on the floor against the side of our suede couch.
Nanay and Tatay sit on the plush seats. On TV, Whitney Houston
is about to kiss her bodyguard.

"Vangie, Acon, turn around." Nanay and Tatay always make us
turn around when people on TV kiss.

"Nanay?"

"*Ano* (What)?"

"Nanay, maybe I came out of Tatay's belly instead? Maybe that's why I don't look like you and Ate?"

Tatay chokes and coughs. Ate slaps me on the hand and laughs. Nanay stares at me and squeaks, "She's your daughter, Val. Tell her. Did she come from you?"

"Of course, that's why she's good looking like me!" Tatay curls three fingers, sticks his pointy finger in the air and then places it under his chin. "We're cute!"

Tatay flashes me a grin and rises from the couch. He pads barefoot across the parquet floor down the hall to the bathroom. I jump up, run across the hall, and stop in front of the closed bathroom door.

"Tatay?"

"Yes?"

"How much longer are you gonna be in there?"

"I'm pooping. I don't know."

Plop.

"Vangie, what are you doing?" Nanay screams from the living room.

"Waiting for Tatay," I shout.

I say his name again. "Tatay?"

"Yes, Vangie?"

Plop. Plop.

"Are you done yet?"

"No."

"Tatay, I miss you. Come out now!"

"Vangie, I'm pooping!"

Plop. Plop. Plop.

"I know, but you're taking too long. I miss you!"

I hear the toilet flush. I hear the water run. The door clicks open.

I look up and smile at Tatay. He dries his hands on a white ter-rycloth towel. Tatay laughs, ruffles my hair, and picks me up into his arms.

Chocolate

Afreen Chowdhury

Thirty second-graders with pink noses and flushed cheeks walk single file down the hallway of Oakridge Elementary School. *Clog. Clog.* Our Disney and superhero winter boots march. Snow and slush slide down my purple snow pants and onto the tiled floors. The large brown doors lock behind us. I frown.

I enter the class and walk to the back of the room. Two rows of small cubbies wait for little hands to stuff them with wet hats and dirty mitts and scarves. I stand in front of my cubby and begin to remove layers of winter clothes. I take off my soggy, purple cotton gloves with glitter stars. My red hands sting from the cold. I yank off my hat, scarf, snow pants, boots and winter jacket. They drip with snow water. A puddle on the floor splashes my jeans as a classmate runs by. I wrinkle my nose.

"Please, quickly sit down at your desks!" Mr. Atkinson says.

I sit down at my desk. Maps and handdrawn pictures of people, animals and places fill the wall on my left. Giant windows take up most of the wall at my right. I watch as the last of my classmates reach their desks. I face the front again, dangle my feet, and wait for the teacher's instructions.

"Today is Wednesday!" Mr. Atkinson says. "That means it is show and tell time. Please take out your show and tell. Then, sit down quietly on the big rug."

Mr. Atkinson smiles and sits down on the wooden rocking chair next to the big rug.

My mouth breaks into an open smile. Show and tell happens every other Wednesday. I mark down the dates on my kitty calendar and then choose the toys I want to bring. But today I forgot.

All my classmates crowd at the back of the class and take out their show and tell. I sit at my desk with elbows on top and chin in my hands.

There has to be something here that I can use for show and tell. I search around and inside my desk. I spot a yellow pencil, workbooks and a mini M&M's container. I pick up the tube-like container. It's half full of mini M&M's candies. I smell the chocolate, then shake the container and listen to the M&M's rattle inside. I get an idea—I'll pretend this is a musical instrument. If anyone becomes suspicious, I can say it's an object from my culture.

Most students sit at the front of the class on the large, round rug with rings of colour like a jawbreaker candy. Almost everyone holds something for show and tell. I sit down and keep mine hidden between my crossed legs.

I wonder if anyone will be able to tell it's just an M&M's container.

Mr. Atkinson moves his finger around the circle. "Let's begin from that end and we will go around this way!"

The first boy explains his toy. "This is my favourite car. My brother bought it for me for my bir—" His voice fades as I look back at the container. It still has the M&M's label on it. My eyes widen. I rip off the label and sit on it.

I look at Mr. Atkinson. What if he thinks I'm a bad student? I chew on the inside of my mouth.

Half the students around the circle have made their presentations. My stomach begins to hurt. It hurts more as the turns pass on. I look at the M&M's container. I look at the person presenting.

I should not show it. Should I? My hands sweat. I think I should, maybe.

My turn nears.

I rehearse what to say. *This is a musical instrument from my country. It's like a rattle. This is a musical instrument from my country. It's like a rattle.* No one else in my class comes from Bangladesh, so no one should know that I'm lying.

"Afreen, it's your turn." Mr. Atkinson beams at me.

My face feels hot. I swallow the little bit of spit I have in my dry mouth. "I brought this." I hold up the blue mini M&M's container.

My stomach drops.

"This is a traditional musical instrument from my country."

I shake the container. My stomach drops more.

"It makes noise when you shake it like this."

I gaze around the circle and then at my teacher. Mr. Atkinson smiles a crooked smile. I put my lie back on my lap. I peer up at Mr. Atkinson again. He stares down at me. Then he looks away.

Away Game

Lauren Tashiro

I hate away games.

Dad slams the trunk shut. I buckle up my seatbelt and hold my breath. Mom starts the car. She looks in the rearview mirror at me. Her blue eyes flit away as she runs a hand through her brown-blonde hair. Outside, streetlights illuminate the road and the snow whirling to the ground.

Dad clambers into our silver Toyota Highlander. It rocks under his weight. He slams the door.

I shudder. I drop my head and swallow. Mom starts the car, backs out of the parking spot and exits the lot of Lions Arena in Kitchener. The car is quiet; not even the radio is on. Mom always has the radio on. I grip the swishy black pants of my team uniform. I'm glad that I sit behind Dad. I don't have to see his face.

We drive down the road for a few minutes. Dad turns in his seat and looks down at me. His dark eyes narrow. His forehead wrinkles, bringing his receding hairline forward.

Dad clears his throat.

Here it comes.

"Well, you played like crap," he growls. "Seven goals? Really?"

My jaw tightens. My heart beats fast in my chest. I shove my hands under my thighs.

"Kelvin," Mom interrupts. She glances at him. Her eyebrows furrow.

Snow still drifts to the ground.

"No Colleen, she played like crap!" Dad turns back around in his seat and faces forward. All I can see is the top of his curly black hair.

"It takes a whole team to play hockey!" Mom says.

"Lauren has to learn from her mistakes!" Dad retorts. "She'll never be a good goalie if she doesn't learn."

He turns back toward me. "For the first goal, you didn't have your glove up! And the second and third goals? Right through your five hole! You have to butterfly! Snap your knees! Don't be lazy!

"For the other goals, you tell me what you did wrong!"

I swallow again. My throat burns. I open my mouth to speak, but nothing comes out.

"Well?" Dad shouts.

Dad has never played a single game of hockey in his life, yet he thinks he'd do better? I'd never say that, though. Never.

"The fourth goal, I didn't slide fast enough. The fifth goal, I wasn't square to the puck. The sixth goal, I didn't control my rebound. I...I can't remember the seventh goal."

"The seventh goal you didn't T-push fast enough!"

"Yes," I choke. My lips tremble. The tears come.

Dad continues to list everything I did wrong, and how I need to improve.

I sniff and wipe my tears.

"Kelvin, that's enough!" Mom screams.

Dad scoffs. But he doesn't say another word.

The car is silent. The snow has stopped.

I hate away games.

Piss

Sara Middleton

I wake up and feel the wetness beneath me. I scramble out of bed. The clock reads 5:56. I have half an hour until he wakes up. I can't believe I did it again.

I strip off my piss-soaked pyjamas and change into fresh clothes. I rip the sheets and blanket from the bed and use the dry parts to soak up the wet spots on the mattress. I toss the wet stuff on the floor and edge the window open to air out the room. The window squeaks. I listen for a sound from down the hall. I hear only my heart beating. I gather the soiled linens and cautiously open the door.

I pause at the top step, feel reassured when I hear snoring from down the hall, then tiptoe down the stairs. I toss the sheets into a pile in the far corner of the laundry room—I'll deal with them after school—and grab fresh ones. I go back to my bedroom, flip the mattress over and put the clean sheets and blanket on the bed. I mess it up a little to look like it's been slept in. I grab Febreze from the kitchen and spray it lightly around the room.

I go to the bathroom and clean myself up. I get back to my room and hear the house begin to wake for the day. I hear Mom head to the bathroom. I peer around the door of my room and see Dad coming towards me on his way to the kitchen.

Terror runs through me. I stare at the floor. His feet stop inches away. I look up. His face contorts in disgust.

"You pissed yourself again, didn't you?"

My eyes meet the floor again.

"This is why you have no friends. You don't deserve friends."

Dad walks to the kitchen. I turn around and slowly close my door. My cat, Red, sneaks inside before it shuts. I sit on the bed and cry. Red snuggles against me.

I wait until Dad leaves for work. I put my hair up in a ponytail and pull on jeans and a T-shirt. I eat a piece of toast. I don't tell Mom what happened. It's best not to.

I head out the door. Red follows me. I shoo him away. The other kids will think I'm weird. Red dodges from bush to bush, trailing behind me almost all the way to school. I lose sight of him as I cross the school parking lot.

The bell rings. I line up with the other fifth graders. Our teacher, Mrs. Eaton, leads us to our classroom. What if they can smell pee on me? The other kids chatter with their friends. Mrs. Eaton tells them to quiet down. I sit at my desk near the back of the class. The desk next to mine, Kayla's desk, sits empty. I feel disappointment and relief.

Mrs. Eaton takes attendance. Kayla, late again, walks through the door with her shock of red hair. She takes her seat beside mine. I smile hesitantly. Kayla refuses to meet my eyes. Cold dread runs through me. Once class begins, Kayla rips a piece of paper from her notebook, writes something, and passes it to me.

"I'm mad at you," the note says.

I'm not sure what I did. But I have to make it better. My hand shakes as I write back and tell her I'm sorry.

Kayla writes another note. "If you don't make it up to me, I'm going to tell everyone your secret."

A few weeks ago, Kayla came to play at my house. She said she smelled something funny in my room. I told her the truth.

At recess, Kayla tells me I have to cancel my plans with Gemma tonight and tell Gemma, my only real friend, I don't want to see her anymore. She says this will make up for whatever I did to her. I beg Kayla to make it anything else.

"If you don't do it, Sara, I'm going to tell everyone you wet your bed like a little baby. If you don't come and play with me after school, I'm going to hurt myself." I've seen Kayla repeatedly bang her head on the metal frame of her bed. "I do that when you make me angry."

The bell rings. It's time for gym class. I promise Kayla I'll find Gemma next recess and tell her she's not my friend anymore.

I dread gym. I feel exposed. I hate undressing in the change rooms. I never know what to wear, and I hate exposing my body to the other girls. I lie to a couple of the girls and say I need to use the washroom. I change there. We get to the gym and sit in a circle. My hips are disjointed and I can't sit cross-legged like the other kids. I feel stupid. Teachers always nag me to sit properly. I wish I could. I'm comfortable only with my legs to the side.

Before I sit down, the PA beeps for an announcement. We all listen. "Mr. Bole? Can you please send Sara down to the office?"

Everyone stares. My face flushes. I keep my head down and grab my bag and walk to the office. I peer through the glass door, afraid to knock. One of the secretaries, Mrs. Doyle, meets my eyes and motions me to enter. A small fourth grader sits in a chair and holds Red on her lap. Red looks ready to bite and tear at the kid. Red jumps out of the kid's arms and struts over to me. I pick him up. Mrs. Doyle looks at me, amused.

"This is the third time we've caught your cat walking down the halls of the school," she says. "He seems to be looking for you."

I stare at the floor and mumble, "I'm sorry."

I ask if I can take Red home. Mrs. Doyle says yes. She knows I live just around the corner. "Come right back to school."

I clutch Red to my chest and walk out the doors. Red purrs. I kiss him on his head. Tears flow from my eyes.

I don't go back to school.

Willie Lavigne

Laurie Kallis

W illie Lavigne appears midway through grade five.
Willie Lavigne rides a ten-speed bike.

Willie Lavigne has long dirty blond hair.

I do not fit in well at Warren Park Public School, especially with the girls. I fare better with the boys, as long as I stay at the edge of their activities. That's where Willie Lavigne finds me, behind the cage of the baseball diamond.

I come early every morning, before school begins. With my face pressed against the cool chain-link fence, I watch the guys practise. Nobody bothers me. The guys silently accept me there, where the limestone screening meets the grass, where I first meet Willie Lavigne.

"Girls don't belong here." Willie Lavigne's first words break the early morning calm. I say nothing.

Later, in a note I secretly labour over during math class, I declare my right, a girl's right, to hang out wherever I want. On the way to recess, I thrust my note at Willie Lavigne in the stairwell and race down the stairs and out the heavy green door. I feel safe. I won't have to face him for a while. During recess, the boys and girls stay on separate sides of the school.

When the bell rings, I head back upstairs to Mr. Russell's class. Willie Lavigne catches up with me.

"After school," he says, "you're gonna eat your note."

"Okay," I say. "Meet me at the top of the hill."

Everyone clusters around, calling me by name. They want to know what's going on between me and the new boy.

After school, I run all the way up Varsity Avenue and down the steep hill of Warren Crescent to our tall brick house. Word has already travelled to my street. The other kids, even those who go to Humbercrest and to St. Mary's, know something's happening. Without stopping, I blurt out my side of the story, then rush into our empty house. My parents work until almost five.

I brush my tangled hair and share my story with Sluggo, our little black and white dog. Sluggo tilts her head and watches me as I speak.

Sluggo comes with me, and together we stride up the hill. People watch us, from above and below.

Sluggo and I reach the top.

Willie Lavigne kneels down and pats Sluggo's head. "You didn't have to bring your dog. I wasn't really gonna fight you," Willie Lavigne says. "Do you wanna go for a walk?"

I walk my dog. Willie Lavigne walks his ten-speed bike.

That summer, Willie Lavigne is the witness when two teenagers steal my dad's Pontiac Parisienne from outside the Becker's store. They crash into a tree, scraping the bark from its skinny little trunk.

After that, even Dad thinks Willie Lavigne is pretty cool.

Willie Lavigne tells me his mother slipped a *cid* into his coke.

Willie Lavigne says I take great slap shots, for a girl.

Willie Lavigne buys the pictures of horses that I draw.

Willie Lavigne slides down Dead Man's cliff, on his arse.

Willie Lavigne plays his saxophone for me, from the back step of his building.

Then, Willie Lavigne kisses me.

~~~

Willie Lavigne moved away before grade six began. They tore down the Becker's store, but the tree still grows there. I stop sometimes and touch the smooth surface, where Dad's Parisienne ripped away the bark.

Power Rangers

Andrew Ihamaki

I stand in the doorway to the kitchen at seven in the morning, my eyes blurry with sleep. The sun casts an outline of the window onto the floor. The sun-soaked linoleum warms my bare feet. I rub my eyes into focus and watch Mom get ready for work. She mixes instant coffee in a cup—two milks, two sugars.

I want to ask her how she can drink that stuff, but I stay quiet. I know not to bother Mom when she's in a hurry. She stirs the coffee, licks the spoon, and tosses it into the empty sink. The sound of metal on metal rattles throughout the kitchen. Before Mom takes her first sip, I slip into the washroom and close the door. When I'm done, I push the handle on the toilet and slam down the seat. I climb onto the toilet to reach the faucet and scrub my hands with soap and water.

Then I remember. *Power Rangers* is on!

I tiptoe past my bedroom. My older brother Shawn snorts and groans in his sleep. I drag my feet along the brown bristles of the carpet and reach the living room. I plop myself in front of the TV. It's already on but switched to the stupid news. It's Saturday morning—it should be on *Power Rangers*.

The remote rests on the coffee table, right between Mom's pack of du Maurier's and Dad's pack of Player's Light. I reach for the remote and almost tip the ashtray. The mountain of ash and butts looks ready to spill over.

My fingers punch in the numbers 2 and 5.

The TV hisses before the show's familiar theme song plays from the right speaker. I wind up and slap the frame of our top-of-the-line GE floor model TV. The picture flickers briefly. I hear a pop, a screech, and then the left speaker hums and sings along with the right one. The episode is a rerun, but I don't mind. Tommy is my favourite Power Ranger. He's green.

Mom brings me a bowl of Cheerios. I grab the spoon and force as many *o*'s into my mouth as I can. I lick my lips. A small dribble of milk escapes and trickles down. It collects at the tip of my chin and drips back into my bowl. Mom wipes my face with a towel and then rubs the back of my head with her hand.

"Look at this rat's nest you have on your head. It looks like nobody owns you!" Mom loves making this joke about my hair. "Maybe your dad can comb it for you."

Mom always rushes to get ready for work in the morning. She works a lot. Even at night. After I go to bed, I can hear her in the living room getting ready for her other job.

I sit cross-legged on the shag carpet. I scratch my ankles. When some commercials come on, I look around for Mom. Her du Maurier's are gone. I hear her car pull out of the driveway. I sprint to the front door and peek through the window. I wave goodbye. She waves back and points to her eyes, her chest, and then at me. I watch her drive away until she turns the corner down the street. I sit back down in front of my bowl of Cheerios. I look around the room and study the wood panelling and the paintings on the wall. They remind me of Grandma and Grandpa's cottage.

Beth, my sister, sits down on the couch. Her hair tangles in the back, but not nearly as much as mine. She takes off her glasses and digs the sand from her eyes. Beth breathes on the lenses and wipes them with her nightgown. She examines the glasses and props them back onto her nose.

"Beth, why does Mom always have to work on weekends?" I ask.

"She just does."

"Okay," I say.

Beth is smart. She's in grade six. I'm in kindergarten.

The commercials end and my sister gets up and leaves. I watch the action on the screen, but I think about Mom. I wonder why she never watches *Power Rangers* with me anymore, even though she promises. I know Dad can't because he works all night and Mom tells me not to wake him. Shawn and Beth won't watch it with me, either. *Power Rangers* is a boys' show, so Beth isn't allowed to watch it, and Shawn thinks it's stupid.

I think Shawn's stupid.

Green Beans and Barbie Dolls

Samantha Ashenhurst

S tephanie, grab me a Coke and then we're going," barks Steph's
dad as he lights up another cigarette on the concrete steps in
front of their semi-detached house on Willow Way. He smokes with
his head resting against the palm of his hand.

It's a humid July morning. I've spent most of summer vacation
with my best friend, Steph. We're eleven and start grade six in
September. Steph's grandfather owns a large farm about an hour
away from our Mississauga homes. He specializes in exotic animals.
His farm has emus and llamas and pigs and cows. Her grandfather,
though old, is strong. He has a thick German accent and kind eyes.
He is Steph's favourite person in the world and the only one she
allows to call her "Stephie."

Steph's father works nights. He's always tired during the day.
Sometimes Steph's father nods off at the dinner table while talking
to Steph's mother. Steph doesn't talk about her dad much, but when
she does, she calls him "a bastard." I never know how to respond.

Steph runs inside to fetch her dad's Coke. I stand awkwardly in
her driveway and watch her mom buckle Tara, Steph's five-year-old
sister, into the back seat. Then her mom goes back inside the house
to grab their cocker spaniel, Dolly.

Steph's dad continues smoking his cigarette.

The sun warms the back of my neck.

The air smells of sweat and coconut sunblock.

The Honda doesn't have a working air conditioner. The drive to Norval will be unpleasant with a full car.

Steph comes back outside and hands her dad the can of Coke. He takes it without thanking her. She turns and runs back toward the house. Steph's dad stubs out his cigarette and calls out after her. "Stephanie, where're you going? Grandma's making us lunch. We gotta go, now!"

"Just a sec!" she yells. "I'm getting my knapsack." Steph hurries into the house.

We've secretly started playing with Barbies again, something we haven't done since kindergarten. We need to bring our dolls so that we can play with them in the tall grass next to her grandparents' house.

Steph's mom comes out with Dolly, places her on the back seat with Tara, and stands next to the driver's side of the car. Steph's dad shuffles over to the car and stands next to her. He takes his keys from his pocket and plays with them. I stand near the trunk and wait for Steph.

Steph comes out and hustles toward the car. Her purple plastic sandals snap on the pavement as she walks. She carries her small knapsack in her left hand.

"Okay, get in the car," Steph's dad says. "We gotta get moving if we're gonna be on time."

"Fuck, I'm hurrying, okay?" Steph mutters in a low voice.

Steph's dad moves quickly. In an instant, he has her pinned to the car door, the collar of her shirt bunched in his left hand. His face is red and his body rigid. His right fist is pulled back, ready to strike. Steph's mom grabs his arm. "Doug, stop it, goddamn it! Get away from her!"

"Just let me hit her once!" he spits. His angry voice rings through the quiet summer street.

I don't move. I stare at my best friend, pinned to the hot car. Steph's face, initially marked with surprise, has a look of complete disgust. She doesn't say anything. She just watches her dad's face. Steph's mother curses her husband. Her dad lowers his fist. He releases his grip on Steph's Club Monaco T-shirt. Tara sobs loudly inside the car. Dolly barks at us through the open window. We stand quietly for a beat. Steph's dad steps back and looks at the ground. He looks away from his daughter's eyes. Steph stares at him. I still haven't moved.

"Alright, girls, get in the car." Steph's mom sighs. "Gramma and Grampa are waiting for us."

We ride in silence for the next hour. Steph stares out the open car window, her face blank. Sweat collects on her brow. She doesn't wipe it away. Dolly sits wedged between Tara and me. I rub the dog's curly brown hair as Steph's father drives.

We arrive at Steph's grandparents' house shortly after lunchtime. Her grandfather greets us on the porch with kisses to our cheeks, and tells us that lunch is almost ready. He hands us a basket and asks us to pick some fresh green beans from the garden to have with lunch. Steph and I walk behind the house toward the garden, kicking pebbles. The summer heat intensifies the smell of manure.

As we silently pick green beans together, I hear Steph utter under her breath, "Fucking bastard."

Chapter 2: School

*Present a short, detailed account
of an experience you had in school.*

The Calculus Test

Mike DeLellis

B ooks and study notes cover the kitchen counter, accounting on the left and economics on the right. My calculus text, solution manual, photocopied handouts and copies of old tests, lie scattered on one end of the kitchen table. Solutions to assigned homework sprawl on the other end and fill two kitchen chairs.

I have worked on calculus for three days. The clock on the stove shows two-thirty. The test starts at four.

I write out an answer to a problem. Mom walks in and stands between the counter and the table. She shakes her head and frowns. "Mike, look what you've done to my kitchen. Can't you be a little neater? Can't you?"

"Don't worry about the kitchen, Mom. I'll clean up when I finish studying. I have my calculus test today and my accounting final on Monday. After that, I'll clean the kitchen."

Mom picks up a pile of accounting notes. "Can't I throw some of these out? If someone comes, I'll be embarrassed."

"No, Mom. I can't throw anything out. I've been writing tests all week. Another four days won't make a difference."

Mom lays the notes back on the counter. "Alright, you better get ready for school."

"Okay, just one more question. I should do all right. I understand all of the homework the professor assigned and he said half the test will come straight from the homework. I've studied hard."

I finish the question, then get up, wash my face, comb my hair, and dress. I put on what I wear for every test—black shoes, black socks, black jeans, a black T-shirt, a blue jean shirt and my blue U of T hat. I grab my black school bag and put on my coat.

"Mom, I'm going! Be home around five-thirty."

Blowing snow makes driving difficult. I don't care. I feel good. I should do well on this test. I know the material.

I arrive at UTM's Kaneff Centre at 3:45. Teaching assistants let students into the lecture hall. I walk in, put down my things, take my pencil case and student card out of my bag, and look for a seat. A friend, Fabio, sits near the back. He rests his head on his arms, eyes closed. I sit down next to him.

"Fabio, wake up!"

He lifts his head. He looks pale with dark bags under his eyes.

"Fabio, are you feeling all right?"

"Yeah, I'm just tired. I didn't start doin' the homework until yesterday."

"How much sleep did you get?"

"Sleep? What's sleep? Do people still do that?"

"Fabio, are you crazy? How could you not sleep at all?"

"Desperation, Mike. Desperation can make you do things you wouldn't believe were possible. Trust me, I know."

"Are you ready for this test?"

"I think so. How about you?"

"I think I'll do okay."

I look at my watch—4:08.

"Alright, put everything away," says Mrs. Geddes, who taught me everything I know about calculus but didn't teach this course. "I'm going to hand out the tests now."

She gives a stack of test papers to three supervisors who hand them out. "Did anyone not receive a test paper?" asks Mrs. Geddes. "Alright then, the test is out of fifty marks. It is now 4:12. You have fifty minutes to write. You may begin."

I turn over the paper. I read the first question and know the answer from the homework.

4:22. I complete the first question. I feel confident I got the full five marks. I smile.

4:30. I know the answer to the second question from studying. I finish the second question. I want to finish the test. I want to get a perfect score. I glance at Fabio. Scratch-outs fill his paper. I feel bad for him.

4:32. The third question is worth forty out of the fifty marks. Forty marks! The prof made one question worth eighty percent of the test. I read the question. I do not understand it. It has six parts: A, B, C, D, E and F. I don't know the answer to any of them.

4:38. I read the question again. My heart beats fast. Sweat forms on my upper lip. I do not know what to do.

4:42. I look around the room. Students stare at the walls, the ceiling and the floor.

4:45. Fabio calls a teaching assistant, hands in his paper, and walks out.

4:48. About a quarter of the class has handed in their papers and left.

4:50. I get an idea about parts A, B and C. I write. I write and write.

5:00. I finish the answers to A, B and C. I don't know if they're right. I have five minutes left to answer the last three parts. I scrawl formulas on the test paper.

5:05. "Everybody stop!" Mrs. Geddes says. "Please stay seated until we collect and count your papers."

The teaching assistants collect the papers. I walk down the steps, pick up my bag and coat, and head to the cafeteria. I see students from the calculus test. One sits on a chair, hands on her face, and cries. Her tears spread mascara. A friend offers a tissue. She wipes her eyes and runs to the washroom. Another student stands at one of the pay phones against the wall and yells into the phone, "I didn't know what the fuck I was doing! The fuckin' prof assigned forty fuckin' marks out of fifty for one fuckin' question. Can you fuckin' believe that?"

My friends sit in chairs just across from the Harvey's.

"Mike, what took you so long?" Bruno says. "We've been here for twenty-five minutes."

"That was the hardest test I've ever written," I say. "I can't believe it. I studied hard, really hard, and now I'm just hoping to pass."

"Mike, none of us answered the third question," Bruno says. "Do you know what that means? That means the most we can get is twenty percent."

"Fabio, didn't the prof tell our class that half the test would come from the homework?"

"Mike, you don't get it. They're out to hurt us. Two out of the three questions came from the homework, but they count for only twenty percent of the mark. The prof tricked us."

"How do you think you did?" I ask Fabio.

He shakes his head. "I didn't get past the first question, Mike. I didn't get past the first question."

Sunday Afternoon

Paul Maka

The sound of a car pulling into the driveway takes my mind out of the world of Robertson Davies. A blue pen and a green highlighter rest on my knee. The car door slams shut. I close the book and listen. No voices. Dad must be home. My Sunday afternoon study period ends.

I hear his boots thud up the front porch steps, then the kicking off of salt and slush. The screen door creaks open. Keys rattle. He always tries at least seven before finding the right one. The dead bolt slams back, the door swings open. The alarm box in the hall sounds its computerized warning beeps.

"Hello? Hello? Is anyone home?" Dad takes a few steps into the hall. "What are you doing in there?" He stands at the doorway.

I sit in the living room, the quietest and most comfortable room in the house. "I have to finish this book for class tomorrow."

He grunts and walks away.

I pick *Fifth Business* back up. The main character was killed by the usual cabal: himself, first of all; by the woman he knew; by the woman he did not know; by the man who granted his innermost wish; and by the inevitable fifth, the denouement.

Who were the two women? I flip back a few pages and start to reread a selection.

"Oh, Paul, don't rest your feet on there! What are you doing?"

Dad stands in the doorway again. My feet rest on the solid oak coffee table. I feel comfortable.

"Can you leave me alone? I'm trying to get some work done!"

He walks away and mutters, "Work? That's work?" His sarcastic laughter trails from the room.

I grab my books, pen and highlighter and storm down the basement stairs. The only English class Dad took was designed for engineers. He laughs when he tells the story. "We never even read the book. We all just copied off the smart guys. Ha. They just sat there in the cafeteria with their notebooks spread open on the table and we stood around writing everything down. You didn't have to do any work and you still passed."

I am in the English Specialist program at UTM. I have to read at least four books a week just to keep up.

I turn on my computer. The fan whirs and the tower vibrates. I wedge a book up against it to stop the noise. Upstairs, Mom arrives home. I hear Dad yell at her. He complains about my little brother Michael.

"All he ever does is watch TV."

I know this song. I can't hear Mom's tired response. It doesn't matter. It's the same fight every day. Michael maintains a B average in school.

I flip open my notebook and find my assignment: Write a detailed account of family life. I type a few points.

"...and what about Paul? I never see him doing any work. All he does all day is play computer games. What kind of courses does he take? I wish I had classes like that when I was in university."

Dad comes down to check up on me as I type my essay. The screensaver comes on when I stop to think. He thinks screensavers are computer games. My heart pounds. My hands tremble. I want to yell something at him. Instead, I write.

My Last Presentation

Phillip Parsons

M y grade twelve English teacher tells us to write an essay and prepare a presentation on two books. I choose *A Farewell To Arms* by Ernest Hemingway and Erich Maria Remarque's *All Quiet on The Western Front*. Both are antiwar novels.

"Along with a summary of your essays, you have to present a creative component, something that will make your presentations different," Ms. Kwasnica adds.

My heart sinks.

The presentations will take place in the library where we have access to PowerPoint. Great. More than just my twenty-five class-mates will be watching me.

I'm a pretty creative guy. I've been writing songs for the past year. One, "For The Empire," is a narrative about a famous World War I battle. In it, a soldier from Newfoundland fights on behalf of Britain in The Battle of Beaumont Hill, where many Newfoundland soldiers lost their lives. I contemplate singing the song in front of the class. That's crazy, I think. Sing in front of people who have known me for four years but barely know me at all?

Two nights before my presentation, I strum my beige Norman acoustic guitar in my room. Two and a half years ago, my folks bought me the guitar for Christmas. I'd asked for it on a whim.

In bed, I weigh the pros and cons of singing the song. I will go through with it. *But what if something goes wrong?* I won't see these people for very much longer. *But what if something goes wrong?*

I'd rather leave school knowing I had tried and failed than to leave knowing I didn't try at all. *But what if something goes wrong?*

The next day in the library of Iona Catholic Secondary School, I watch my classmates' presentations. One reads a poem from a book. Another slips a disc into the CD player and a song blares from the speakers. Oh, they'll hear a song tomorrow, I tell myself.

After school, I race home and practise for three hours. I play my song until every word and chord is burned into my memory.

> *For The Empire I will risk my life,*
> *and for proud Newfoundland I will sacrifice.*

My parents come home and I rush to the door to tell them. "I'm going to sing a song in school for my project."

Mom looks at me. "Really? That's great. Better go and practise."

At ten, I slip into bed. I cannot fall asleep. I go over the words again and again.

> *I will die so the world will remain free,*
> *I'll fight for the Empire and I'll fight for me."*

I fall asleep at one.

The next morning I dry heave as I wait for seven-thirty to arrive. I grab my guitar and backpack and head for the car. Every few steps I pause and throw up air. If I had eaten breakfast, it would be splattered across the floor.

"Phillip, why don't you just read the song," Mom says to me in the driveway.

"No."

I open the car door, toss the guitar in the back, and slump into the front seat. Mom starts the car and we're off. It feels like we're only driving five miles an hour. Red lights last for hours and no green lights shine. I mouth the lyrics over and over.

Everyone goes over the top, We're all getting mowed down.
By Jerry's machine guns, And from bombs all around.

We get to the school and Mom parks the car. "Good luck, Phillip," she says. "I'll wait here to pick up your guitar after class."

"Alright," I say and exit the car. I walk to the side doors of the school with my guitar case in hand. My body shakes. My hands tremble. I wobble. I whisper my song until I reach the library.

We finally make it to safety, but there's none of us left.
What is the Empire doing? They are committing theft.

Most of my classmates sit at large tables at the back of the library. Other students fill every desk and chair in the room. I no longer care.

I sit at a desk with my guitar. Ms. Kwasnica sees it and furrows her brow. She starts the class and sets my presentation to be last. I pray for the other presentations to take up the whole period, bleeding the time Ms. Kwasnica has booked for the class.

Andy sets up PowerPoint and presents on two novels about the apocalypse. Evelina talks about relationships between mothers and daughters and plays a Dixie Chicks song on a CD player at the end.

"Phillip, you're up," Ms. Kwasnica says.

I look at the clock. Thirty minutes remain. I grab my guitar and slowly step in front of the class. I place my guitar down and speak about the two books and their antiwar connection. That takes eight minutes.

"Uh, now I'm going to sing a song I wrote."

"Alright," Ramero yells from the back of the room.

"It's called 'For The Empire' and it's about The Battle of Beaumont Hill in World War I."

Even the library staff stop and watch. My mind isn't thinking anymore; it's laughing, laughing, laughing. I sit down, take the guitar from its case, and place it on my knee. The steel strings stretch tight and ready. My guitar pick, which I've named Red Devil, has the perfect bend to play the chords as one sound but enough strength to play the chords with force.

I strum A minor. I stop.

"I'm sorry if I can't sing," I tell the class.

Everybody laughs.

I start to play again.

I sing my song and play my guitar with feelings I didn't know I had. I don't care if it sounds good and I don't care about my grade. My hands on the neck of the guitar sprint from string to string and note to note. I scan each classmate's face. Everything from inspired gapes to bored yawns look back at me.

For the Empire, I will do nothing more.

Almost done now, just a few more lines. My throat is dry, my lips parched, my hands sweaty. I swallow saliva to help my throat finish.

The next day eight hundred names are called out,
and only sixty-eight answer back."

I finish and hear applause.

"Did you really write that song, Phillip?" Ms. Kwasnica asks.

I nod my head. "Yeah, I did."

"That was really deep," Andy says from his chair.

"Thanks."

I place my acoustic in its case and walk back to my seat.

The Pantsing

Madeleine Brown

P antsing? What's that?"

A gang of us grade eight girls stand as a tight pack next to our school, Adam Scott Collegiate Vocational Institute.

"I mean it. What is pantsing?" I say again.

"It's when you pull someone's pants down, just all of a sudden, in front of everyone!" Lauren laughs. "Like this—"

Suddenly, she lunges for the waistband of my pants. I dash away.

"Lauren!" I giggle.

"Yeah, Lauren," Kirstyn cries and teasingly reaches out for Lauren's jeans. She pulls her hands back at the last second.

We break from our clump and run around the schoolyard threatening to pants one another. We end up giggling in a pile on the ground.

"I would actually pants someone," Lauren says as the laughter subsides. "I mean it."

"I dare you, then!" I blurt out. "When recess is over and everyone's at their lockers getting stuff for their next class, you pull down some kid's pants."

Silence. Everyone's eyes fall on Lauren. She agrees to the challenge.

The lunch bell rings and we walk into the school. The weight of the dare slows our pace.

"Dylan. He's wearing basketball shorts, so it'll be easy," Lauren states matter-of-factly.

We stand alongside the wall of the main hallway eyeing our classmates as they busily open their lockers and retrieve binders and books. Dylan and I, best friends from senior kindergarten until the end of grade five, spent birthday parties, playdates and recesses together. I swallow nervously. My throat tightens. We wait for someone to speak.

"Lauren, you don't have to do it," I say. "I was just joking. Don't."

"Yeah, no one cares!"

"Forget it. It's stupid."

Lauren suddenly sprints across the hallway, arms outstretched, and pulls Dylan's green shorts to the floor. His baby blue boxers shine in the dimness of the hallway.

Dylan's face reddens. He drops his books and yanks his shorts back up. The excitement of the pantsing comes and goes in a single second. Nobody, amid the bustle of the hallway, even notices. My eyes dart toward the class clown, Kevin Blunck. Nothing. Cameron Oles and Brad MacLeod, two boys in my homeroom class, walk by oblivious. We feel disappointment and relief. Teachers, however, pop out into the hallway from their classrooms, as if they can sense misbehaviour. Disapproval marks their tired faces.

Ms. Scott marches all of us to the principal's office. She drags Lauren, still standing in awe, with us.

No one speaks.

Going to the principal's office usually means reading the daily announcements over the PA system or receiving words of congratulations on good work. I've never had to visit about bad behaviour. My hands feel clammy, my face flushed and hot.

The vice principal, Ms. Russell, calls us into her office. She lectures us on our unacceptable actions. How do we think Dylan feels now? What if we'd been in his shoes? How embarrassing! Her scolding rattles on. We hang our heads and hold back tears.

It gets worse.

Ms. Russell orders each of us to call our parents and inform them of what happened. "Right now."

I feel stupid explaining pantsing to Mom as my friends and the vice principal listen. "It's when you pull someone's pants down, just all of a sudden, in front of everyone," I mumble into the receiver.

Ms. Russell instructs us to report to the office for detention the following day at lunch. We leave in pained silence.

~~~

The janitor greets us coldly when we arrive for our detention. He hands us each a broom and tells us to sweep the parking lot for the entire lunch hour. "Every grain of sand, every piece of garbage."

I stare up at the glowing sun as I sweep through my first and last detention.

Disturbing the Universe

Nikita Pchelin

P ut your full name and two things unique about you on the attendance sheet I'm sending around the room," chirps Ms. Daniels at the beginning of our first grade-twelve English class. "That way I can memorize your names faster. *Chop-chop!*"

"Nikita Pchelin," I scribble on a sheet of lined paper. "I am from Russia and I like squirrels."

After ten years of Russian school, most classes at Philip Pocock Catholic Secondary School in Mississauga bore me. I doodle during Ms. Lammers' math class. Other students struggle with quadratic equations and use calculators to multiply two-digit numbers. My math teacher in Russia christened my Casio calculator "a devil machine," confiscated it on the first day of grade nine, and returned it to me two years later, before I moved to Canada.

After I disassemble and reunite the parts of dusty old training PCs faster than any of my classmates, I sleep through Mr. Juzkiw's computer engineering class. Since 1997, when Dad got my brother and me our first Pentium II, I have routinely replaced computer hard drives, wiped clean Windows 95 and Windows 2000 Server partitions and installed Linux and FreeBSD.

After I show off my knowledge of organic and inorganic chemistry, I grow bored of Mr. Doyle's chemistry class and ignore the fill-in-the-blank, hand-in assignments. I can recite Mendeleev's periodic table by heart, thanks to the tutoring of my brother, a biology and chemistry teacher by training.

But I stay wide awake in Ms. Daniels' English class. After twelve years of studying English, and writing hundreds of Raymond Murphy's *English Grammar in Use* exercises and several mock Cambridge tests, I still scribble notes on a sheet of paper. I revere the *Collins English Dictionary,* which comes to the rescue each time an unfamiliar word stares at me from the pages of *Death of a Salesman.*

Ms. Daniels is four-foot-seven, witty, and loved by everyone in the class, including the most prominent rebels.

"What would you like your mark to be, Nikita?" Ms. Daniels asked me at the start of the school year.

"Mmmm. Wha...What? You are asking me? I...I don't know, Ms. Daniels. I got seventy-five percent last year and I want to do better for my university application and—"

"You are not answering my question, kiddo." She frowned. "It's okay. We can come back to this later."

Around mid-May, we scrutinize T.S. Eliot's poem "The Love Song of J. Alfred Prufrock." We discover deep symbolism and metaphors in every word. Ms. Daniels yelps "utter rubbish!" several times in reaction to another outrageous guess.

The classroom fills with chatter as we wait for our last class on T.S. Eliot's poem to start. Ms. Daniels enters, dragging a high stool behind her. Beaming at us mischievously, she places the chair in the centre of the room and puts a bag of ripe peaches on the seat.

I glance over at my friend Pavlo, who came from Ukraine where he had attended an educational boot camp similar to mine. The grimace on his face indicates a mixture of surprise and disapproval. I nod. I fidget in my chair. My immediate neighbours, Sandrina and Sean, follow Ms. Daniels with their eyes, eyebrows raised.

Ms. Daniels starts reading the poem. She reads slowly, with rhythm, stressing individual words and whole phrases. Entranced by her voice, and hearing the poem for the hundredth time, I silently recite the lines along with her.

"Do I dare disturb the universe?" her voice booms. "Do I dare to eat a peach?"

She stops and stares, in turn, at each one of us. By the time it's my turn, my eyes flicker. Blinking uncontrollably, I try to stare back. Did I miss a question? I glance at my notes, then at Pavlo, look down at my notes again, and by the time I look back up, Ms. Daniels stares at someone else. The room remains silent. People throw expectant glances at Ms. Daniels and puzzled looks at each other.

Ms. Daniels leaps to her feet. She paces the room and jumps into a monologue about the universe and how we are to disturb it and how there are peaches on every peach tree waiting to be eaten.

I stare at Pavlo. He has given up listening and doodles a Ukrainian coat of arms. She goes on and on about peaches and our future, about the paths that might await us, about the hesitation that makes people miss great opportunities.

"I know you will disturb the universe big time, one day. As for now, who dares to disturb the universe in this classroom? Who dares to eat the peach?" It takes five long minutes before Jessica stands up, walks to the stool, picks up a peach and bites into it.

"Good job, Jessica!" Ms. Daniels applauds. "How does it feel?"

"I was not sure what I was supposed to do, but then I decided to go for it. Oh, and the peach is delicious," replies Jessica.

"You see, guys and gals," Ms. Daniels addresses the class. "Even though you all wear the same blue and white uniform, some of you know how to grab the moment by the tail better than others. Don't worry. You still have some time to learn. Now come on, come everyone, grab a peach."

Enjoying my peach moments later, I rock in my chair and look out the window. Outside, the wind rustles the leaves on the silver maple trees.

~~~

"Well, well, well, little squirrel, there you are!" Ms. Daniels greets me a few years after high school graduation. She tells me about the books she has recently read, school politics, and her new students.

"You know, I still punk them every year when we cover Orwell's *1984*. I pick one big tough guy and make him empty his pockets and knapsack in front of the whole class. I then explain to him that he did not have to do that, because he does have some basic rights, even in an English classroom." Ms. Daniels giggles.

I tell her about my successes and failures, about transferring from engineering to computer science, about interning at my dream company, about my graduation, deferred because of the internship. She listens, nods and beams at me.

"No worries, Nikita. I know you will disturb the universe one day."

PATH

Juliver Ramirez

The attendance sheet lists twenty-five names—eighteen boys, seven girls. I slip the piece of paper into my organizer and place my organizer into my backpack. I will get to know these students over the next semester, as their teacher and, maybe, as a friend. At least I hope so.

As the bell rings, I pull the lanyard over my head. The tag shows my name, picture and title: PATH Student 2011. I adjust the lanyard under my collar, straighten the tag and pat it against my chest.

The guidance counsellors at St. Joseph Secondary School designed the "Peers As Teacher Helpers" program for aspiring teachers like me. It's a co-op placement. They place grade twelve students into the subject of their liking to help an associate teacher conduct a class. Ms. Izquierdo specifically requested that I be her PATH student. We will take on her grade ten Applied English class together.

I leave the portables area, enter the stairwell, and leap up the stairs two steps at a time. Since it's my first day, I want to arrive early. "Set a good example for your students" was one of the things the counsellors stressed during PATH training.

I enter Room 305 and find it deserted. Crooked desks, untucked chairs and a teacher's desk occupy the classroom. I set my backpack down beside Ms. Izquierdo's vacant desk. I figure she must be running late. I straighten desks, push in chairs and swat eraser shavings from desktops. I man my post at the door and await my twenty-five students.

A broad-shouldered student, just a bit bigger than me, wanders down the hall. He scans all of the room numbers on the doors. He glances at me from two classrooms away. He slows down and stops in front of me.

"Hey, which class are you looking for?" I ask.

"English with Izz-keer-doe?"

"Izquierdo," I say. "And yeah, this is it. I'm Juliver, your PATH student."

~~~

Pens and pencils scribble at 9:37 a.m. Students are about halfway done the final exam. Jacklyn, Matthew and Justin bow their heads close to their desks and focus on their essays. Kevin peeks around the room, his page blank.

I sit next to Ms. Izquierdo at the front of the class, halfway finished writing thank you cards to my students. I have special messages for each of them. I want all of my students to know what advice and encouragement I have for them.

The night before, I bought treats for the class. I came home late, started writing the cards, and slept in. I had eight done by the time I left for school.

Jacklyn stands up from her seat and hands in her exam. I give her one of the lollipops and her personalized thank you card.

She opens the card and speeds through it. "Aw, thanks Juliver," she whispers.

More and more students stand as the clock nears 10:30. More and more cards leave my desk.

Kevin, always late and a constant troublemaker, is the last student in the room. Memories of Kevin nearly starting a fistfight in class, stealing Darwin's hat, and coming to class high on marijuana, fill my mind. I want to write something that will change his attitude about school forever.

He stands up at exactly 10:30.

"Hey Kevin, wanna hang back for a bit? I'm almost done with your card." All I have so far is "Dear Kevin."

"Nah, screw it, man. I don't want it. Can I just take some of these lollipops since you have extras? Cool? 'Kay, thanks."

Kevin scavenges the table for the flavours he wants. Ms. Izquierdo starts to scold him. "Uh, Kevin? I don't think you can just…."

Kevin pulls the wrapper off a yellow lollipop and sticks the sucker in his mouth. He smirks and flickers his eyebrows as he turns back to his desk. Kevin slaps on his flat-brimmed baseball cap and dons his black Canada Goose vest over his uniform. He leaves the pencil that he borrowed and chewed on during the exam. Kevin yanks open the door. Without looking back, he swaggers out. The door swings back too hard, hits the supplies cabinet behind it, rebounds and clicks back into place.

Ms. Izquierdo and I sit in silence.

The Substitute

Aristotle Eliopoulos

U ghhhhhh! My new locker sucks so bad! I can never fit my
stuff in here!"

"Well, that's what happens when you go to Meadowvale
Secondary School, I mean 'Ghetto-Jail,'" I say. "You get your choice
of all the finer things—the best curriculum, the best lockers and, of
course, the best drugs!"

Jess smirks. "You might have actually just repeated the motto on
our school's crest."

"We have a school crest?"

"Yeah, it's in my locker." She giggles and glances at her watch.
"What are you doing for third period?"

"I have a spare. Why, what's up?"

"I have my sewing class right now. You should sit in on it."

"I don't know. Won't your teacher kick me out?"

"No way! My teacher is away on mat leave, and they haven't
gotten us a permanent replacement yet. It'll probably just be some
substitute. You can probably trick him into thinking you're part of
the class."

We make our way to the classroom. I intend to walk her to the
door and then go in the other direction, but she playfully, yet force-
fully, pulls me into the room with her. I follow her to the table where
she sits with her other friends. Jess introduces me. I wave. I don't
intend on staying longer than two minutes.

"Here," Jess says. "You can sit in Erin's chair."

I glance at the clock and sit down.

"Erin's absent a lot," says a vacant-looking blonde girl who sits beside me.

"Yeah, seriously," says another girl with shaggy bangs and a pink headband. "Erin needs to start showing up, if she wants to pass. She's, like, being really stupid by skipping class all the time."

The girls giggle. I survey my surroundings. I see no other boys in the room. I look at the clock behind me: 11:15 a.m.

"All right, Jess," I say, getting ready to go. "I'm gonna—"

The door slams shut. I jerk around. The substitute teacher appears at the front of the classroom. I gulp. He looks old and dishevelled, frumpy and out of place. He wears pale jeans and a black varsity jacket. On his upper lip sits a bushy moustache. I want to get up and leave, but I can't.

"Jess," I say, eyeing her with anxiety. She remains calm.

Relax," she says. "If he ends up asking you who you are, just say your name is Erin."

"Your friend?" I say, confused.

"Yeah! When he calls her name on the attendance, just say your name is actually Aaron, A-A-R-O-N. Just pretend the office spelled your name wrong on the attendance sheet."

The substitute teacher drops into his chair. He eyes me. His moustache twitches. He barks out each girl's name on the attendance sheet.

"Kelly!"

"Here," says a girl behind me.

"Rachel!"

"Here!" The vacant-looking blonde beside me raises her hand.

"Erin!"

I don't say a word.

When he finishes, he looks at me once again. Then he tosses the paper on the desk in front of him.

"Alright," he says. "According to your teacher, you're supposed to be working through your exercise books." He points to a box of books that sit on the table. "I'm gonna hand out your assigned book and you'll be working on it for the rest of the class. Any questions?"

The class stays silent.

He hands out the books. When he gets to our table, he approaches me. "What book number is assigned to you?"

"Number…four," I say.

"So your name is…Michelle?" He looks at the book sign-up list in his hand.

"Number…thirteen?" I say.

He glares at me. His eyes fill with anger. "You good-for-nothing kid!" he shouts. "You're trying to trick me! What do you think, I'm stupid or something? What is your name?"

"A-a-aris…"

"What?"

"Aristotle."

"Aristotle," he yells with disgust. "You're in trouble now!" He stomps towards the PA system on the other side of the room. He hits the dial to buzz the office. As he waits for someone to answer, he starts to shout again. "Good for nothing kids thinking they can get away with everything! Do you know in some areas of the world, this behaviour would result in a student being tied to a chair and whipped? If only we lived in those countries now, then I would show you—"

"Hello?" the secretary's voice sounds over the PA system.

"Hi. I have a student who claims his name is Aristotle." The substitute sneers at me. "He doesn't belong in this class and I want him to be punished."

"Oh, okay," the secretary mutters. "Send him down."

I take off down the hall. The man continues to glare at me. I disappear around the corner.

I sit in the office and stare at the clock across from me. Thirty minutes have passed, but it feels much longer. The door behind the secretary's desk opens and the vice principal, Mr. Koehnan, walks out. He looks at me and smiles.

"Aris." Mr. Koehnan was my grade ten English teacher before he became vice principal. "What can I do for you?"

"I got sent down here," I say with some embarrassment. "The substitute sent me down because I was in the wrong class."

"You were in the wrong class?" He looks puzzled.

"Yeah."

"Okay. Well, are you sorry about it?"

"Yes! Very!"

"Good! Uh, have a good day." He waves goodbye and goes back into his office.

Before I can get out the door, I spot the substitute in the hallway outside. He walks past the glass door, keeping his gaze on me. His eyes still look angry, his moustache still twitches. He disappears around the corner. I take a deep breath, push through the office door and blend into the crowd of students outside.

Miss Fitzgerald

Ebi Agbeyegbe

I t's almost noon on yet another bright, sunny day at St. Jacobs High School in Lagos, Nigeria. I sit at the back of the room, just the way I like it. A clock ticks away at the front of the class, pictures hang on the walls, writing fills the chalkboard. Students chat quietly.

My friends and I look forward to noon when all grade five students get an hour for lunch. Some of us play in the spacious field before we return to our classes.

Although I sit at the back, I have a great view of Miss Fitzgerald, my favourite teacher. I admire the way she teaches with such passion. Other students glance at the clock, but I enjoy English class the most. I feel comfortable and I like the lessons.

When the bell rings, everyone packs up their stuff and rushes into the hall towards the cafeteria.

"Don't forget to do the readings on chapter five for the next class," Miss Fitzgerald yells.

I wait a few seconds and stand at the back of the class. I think the standard school uniform makes me look presentable—long-sleeved white shirt, green shorts and black shoes. I roll up the sleeves of my shirt and approach Miss Fitzgerald. My body feels hot as I get close. My palms sweat. Only she and I remain in the classroom.

Miss Fitzgerald's head, her long curly hair pulled back in a neat bun, looks down at the table as she grades some papers.

I reach the table, inhale deeply, and then exhale.

"Hi, Miss."

She jerks up slightly. "Hello, John. How may I help you?"

I look around and see the textbook on her desk. "I wanted to ask about the assignment."

She looks at me and smiles. Everything seems to slow down. I feel the hairs on my skin stand up.

"What exactly would you like me to explain about the homework?" She reaches over, opens the textbook, and flips the pages to the assigned chapter.

"I wanted to know what Shakespeare meant in the story when he said, 'O Romeo, Romeo! Wherefore art thou Romeo?'"

Miss Fitzgerald comes closer to show me the quote. When she stands up, I notice her light brown dress. It looks perfect on her. She explains the quote but all I can think about is how nice she smells.

She finishes and says, "Do you understand now?"

"Yes. You really smell nice, Miss."

She smiles wide and says, "Thank you."

I shuffle back to my desk to get my backpack. I tell myself I have to say something else or I'll look lame. I walk past her desk as I leave and say, "I like your dress, Miss."

She grins, gets up from her seat, walks over to me, and kisses me on the cheek.

I take a deep breath, smile and say, "Thank you, Miss."

I run out of the class towards the field to my friends.

For the rest of the day, I think about Miss Fitzgerald. I get home and I decide to write her a poem. I stay awake until two in the morning, perfecting each word.

The next day when English class ends, I wait behind to hand Miss Fitzgerald the poem. As I bring out the poem, Mr. Malcolm, my math teacher, strolls into the class.

He walks over to Miss Fitzgerald's desk and gives her a kiss on the cheek. "Ready for lunch, babe?"

The poem drops from my hand.

Miss Fitzgerald sees me. She heads towards me and appears to utter some words. I pack up my poem, books, pens and glasses. She calls out my name as I storm out of the classroom.

Choke

Christina Hunter

W hat if someone sees us?" I ask.

While all the other grade eight students sit cross-legged in a stuffy auditorium, my friends and I huddle behind the portables of St. Aaron Elementary School. We rub our hands together for warmth, wipe our noses on our sleeves, blow clouds as we speak, and sniffle between words.

"Everyone's at the assembly. No one's gonna see us. Besides, Johnny's watching for teachers," Graham says.

"I'm just not sure this is a good idea," Adam mutters, hands in his pockets.

"Don't be a pussy," Chris says.

Graham spits into the snow. "You said you'd do it. She'll be here any minute, so make up your fucking mind."

"What if something goes wrong?" Adam says.

"It won't."

"How do you know?"

"Because she's done this, like, a million times."

"And nothing's ever gone wrong?"

"Never."

"She's coming," Johnny calls over.

"Does someone else wanna go first? I wanna see what happens," Adam says. He sweats despite the cold.

"What a fag," Chris laughs.

"Guys, don't force him," I say. "If he doesn't wanna do it...."

"Aw, standing up for your boyfriend?"

"He's not my boyfriend."

"How cute."

"He's not my boyfriend. Anyways, Adam, it's no big deal. We've all done it."

"She's here!" Johnny says.

Hoami saunters over, seething with sex and confidence. Beautiful, charming, outspoken and incredibly stupid, she is every eighth grade boy's wet dream. "What's up?"

"Adam's scared." Graham laughs. He crosses his arms so that his biceps bulge.

"I am not. Let's do it."

Hoami signals to Graham and Chris, who move to support Adam. Hoami sashays forward until she is within inches of Adam's face. She runs her tongue across her lips. Adam swallows. She places her hands on his neck, leans in, tilts his head back, and presses on the veins in his neck. He blinks violently. I see the whites of his eyes dart wildly.

One minute passes. Adam reddens.

"Pressing," Hoami soothes. "Hold your breath, don't fight it. Don't fight, don't fight, don't...there you go."

Two minutes pass. Adam's legs tremble.

Three minutes. Adam's eyes roll back.

"Ease him down, guys," Hoami says. "Be careful. Watch his head."

"Pasty little shit, eh?" Chris jokes.

"A lightweight, too," Graham adds. "That was, what? Two minutes?"

"Three," I say.

"About as long as he'd last in bed," Chris snickers.

"Shut up," I say. "He's waking up."

"How ya feeling?" Hoami asks.

"I'm fucking tripping right now." Adam's eyes, glazed and unfocused, roll from the sky to the ground and back to the sky. "Do it again."

"You can't," I say. "Adam, you've got to wait before you can do it again. You have to let the oxygen back into your brain."

"It's fine. I'm fine. I feel great. Do it again."

"You heard him," Graham says.

"Seriously guys, I don't think—"

"Hold him up, then. I can't do it myself."

"Guys, c'mon."

"You got him?" Graham and Chris support Adam's body between them. He slouches in their arms.

"I think you should wait," I say.

"I think you should stop spazzing," Chris spits.

Hoami moves in again. "Three...two...one," she counts. In less than two minutes, Adam's out. He sways, slumps and falls. His body crumples onto the asphalt.

"Shit!"

"What the fuck are you doing?" I shout.

"Sorry! My arm slipped!" Chris says.

"He could crack his fucking skull!"

"He's fine. Relax," says Hoami.

"Both of you, shut up," Graham says.

I look at Adam. My stomach churns. "Why is he twitching like that?" No one answers. "Why is he twitching like that?"

Johnny rushes over from his guard post, cellphone poised and filming.

"I don't think he's okay. Something's wrong. Is he seizing?"

"No," Hoami huffs. "Just wait, it'll stop."

We watch. I hold my breath. I pray.

"See?" Graham shoves me. "He stopped. Problem solved."

"'Kay. But he's supposed to wake up now, right?"

"Just give it a sec."

"How long is it supposed to take?"

"Would you shut the fuck up?"

"Relax," Hoami says.

"Something's wrong."

"Nothing's wrong."

"He's not waking up. Johnny, get a teacher."

"Are you fucking stupid?" he yells. "We'll get suspended."

"What if he dies? We'll go to jail!"

"Shut up," Chris says. "You're spazzing about nothing. He'll be fine."

"He's fucking purple!"

"Would you shut the fuck up so I can fucking think?"

I've never seen Hoami lose her cool. It feels kind of gratifying. Then I look down at Adam. He looks like he's already dead. I taste bile in the back of my throat.

"I'm gonna go get a teacher."

"Don't you dare," Chris says. He turns to Hoami. "What do we do?"

"Fuck if I know. They always just...wake up."

"We should get a teacher," Graham relents.

"Fuck." Hoami's eyes water. "Shit, fuck, fuck. Does anyone know CPR?"

Silence.

"We can't let anyone find out," Johnny says.

Graham takes out his cellphone and dials 911. "We're so fucked."

I run to get a teacher.

~~~

We were suspended for a week. When Graham, Chris, Johnny and I went back to school, we didn't talk about what happened. We didn't talk to each other at all.

Hoami was expelled.

Adam survived.

I learned later that the high Adam experienced resulted from the death of millions of brain cells. I learned later that Adam suffered massive brain trauma. He never came back to school. I never saw Adam again.

Chapter 3: Family

Present a picture of life in the family
by detailing an event or chain of events
you have experienced or observed.

Fire

Laurel Waterman

A delicate silver line runs up the back of Mom's legs from her heels to her calves to behind her knees and hides under her short electric blue suede skirt. She kicks her black pumps off while she rushes around the kitchen. Cupboards bang, dishes clink, the pan sizzles and the fridge hums as she sidesteps me playing on the kitchen floor.

"Okay. We've got buns, cheese, the burgers—shit!" She steps over me to the burning President's Choice patties and fumbles around the drawer for a flipper.

"Brenda, have you seen my keys anywhere?" Dad shouts from upstairs.

"No, Jay," Mom yells. "Why would I know—shit!" Mom purses her lips and studies her red middle fingernail. "Damn." She rips the broken nail off with her teeth and sucks her finger for a moment.

"Mummy." I point to the smoking pan. Mom scrapes at the burgers and flips them. The meat hisses and smokes more.

NEE-ER NEE-ER NEE-ER. The smoke alarm wails. I cover my ears. Mom rushes to the sink and reaches over to open the window. Her tummy lands in a puddle on the counter.

"Shit!" Mom fishes in the drawer, finds a clean black and white checkered dish towel and tries to dry the dark wet spot on the front of her suede skirt. *NEE-ER NEE-ER NEE-ER.* Mom clicks her teeth and returns to fighting with the window.

"You okay down there?" Dad yells from upstairs. Mom mutters something. Before she can answer, we hear shouts from the third floor.

"FIRE," screams Ryan, my eleven-year-old brother, as he stampedes down the stairs. Aaron, nine, and Neil, five, follow. Now they all scream. "FIRE FIRE FIRE FIRE FIRE."

"Ryan, stop being ridiculous," Mom shouts over the alarm.

Ryan skids across the black and white linoleum floor. "FIRE," he keeps yelling. "Don't worry, Gopher. I'll save you."

Ryan picks me up and throws me over his shoulder.

I scream and pound his back with my fists and kick with my heels. "Put me down, Ryan! It hurts!"

"It's gonna be okay. I've got you." Ryan runs into the living room, lets me down, opens the first-floor window and vaults onto the rockery below. He looks up at me and opens his arms. "Jump, Gopher. I'll catch you." I look back. Mom's not there. "Jump, Gopher, or die in the fire."

Aaron and Neil run out the front door and wrestle on the lawn. The alarm wails. I teeter onto the windowsill. "Jump, sis."

I fall forward and Ryan grabs me. He carries me down the rock garden. "Saved your life."

Ryan drops me on the grass. Aaron pulls me into the wrestling match and gives me a noogie. "Stop," I scream in the same pitch as the alarm. "No," I yell. "They're tickling me and it hurts. Tickling really hurts, guys. Stop it. MOMMY."

The smoke alarm stops.

"Dinner," Mom hollers from the kitchen.

The boys race inside. I toddle in after them. Aaron dives for the buns. "Wait. Hands, please," Mom says.

The boys scamper off to the washroom.

I look at my hands, decide they're clean, and sit at the table in my seat at Mom's right.

Mom carries a tray of condiments and adds ketchup, mustard, relish and mayo to the buns, burgers and cheese already on the table. She's wearing her black pumps again and she looks perfect. Her hair ends flip outward and sit on her lacy black shoulders. She stands behind me, places a burger on my plate, leans over me, and cuts the patty into small pieces.

"Mom, Ryan splashed me," Neil cries from the washroom.

"Boys, right now."

They file in, Neil sulky, Aaron bored, Ryan smiling. Neil sits next to me, Aaron across from me and Ryan next to him. They rock in the creaky wooden chairs and balance on the chairs' back legs. Ryan grabs a bun out of the basket and tosses it at Neil. Half falls on the floor.

"Ryan," Mom says, "quit it."

Dad trots down the stairs and sits at other end of the table. He smells like Old Spice aftershave. Dad pats Neil on the head and serves himself. Mom finishes cutting my burger, sits down, sighs, and closes her eyes for a moment.

"Pass the burgers please, Jay." Dad picks up the plate and hands it to Ryan, who shoves it at Aaron, who passes it to Mom. "Thank you. Ryan, could you please pass the mayo?"

Ryan picks up the open mayonnaise jar and whips it down the middle of the table. It knocks over the bun basket, smashes into my glass, falls off the end and spills onto Mom's lap.

No one moves.

Mom looks down and breathes loudly. Ryan freezes, poised to jump, watching her. Dad sits stunned and thinks of what to say.

Mom jumps out of her chair and lunges at Ryan. Ryan takes off up the carpeted stairs. Mom chases him in her heels, mayonnaise globs dropping from her skirt. The stairs creak violently. We hear a muffled thud-thump, thud-thump and a door slam.

"Ryan!" Mom screams. "Open this door this instant!"

Ryan keeps the door locked. Minutes pass. I poke at the burger pieces on my plate.

We hear someone coming down the stairs. Dad, Neil, Aaron and I look at each other. Mom hobbles into the room with a bleeding knee, ripped stockings and messy hair.

Dad stands up. "Are you okay, Brenda?"

Mom whispers through her teeth, "That kid is smart. If he had opened that door, I would have killed him. I would have killed him. I swear I would have thrown him out the window."

The doorbell rings. Mom sighs. "It's the babysitter. You let her in. I'm going to change."

I crawl upstairs to help Mom pick out a new outfit.

The Perfect House

Shane Driver

M y older brother sits on the curb crying in front of our new
house. Eric's thirteen, I'm eleven.

"What's the matter?" I ask.

"Shut up and leave me alone." Eric is usually tough as hell, always
getting into fights. He never cries.

"C'mon," I say. "Tell me."

"I don't want to move into this shithole."

The new house in Oakville is much larger than our old house in
Newmarket. On a corner lot with a basketball net, two-car garage
and a big backyard, it looks like a mansion.

"This isn't a shithole," I say.

"Shut the fuck up. You're an idiot!"

At five-thirty in the evening, the October air feels cool and the
orange sun sets deep in the western sky as we help Dad carry in the
last boxes.

Dad leaves to drive the U-Haul truck back to the depot and pick
up some take-out from Swiss Chalet. Mom doesn't feel like fixing
supper. She peers out the kitchen window and sees Eric and me sitting on the curb. Mom looks concerned.

"Why are you so pissed off?" I ask Eric.

"I liked Newmarket. All my friends were there and pretty soon
Mom and Dad are going to get a divorce."

My focus quickly changes.

"What do you mean?" I don't let Eric answer my question. "They are not. I don't think they are."

"That's because you're an idiot."

Mom and Dad do fight a lot. They wanted out of Newmarket because Eric got into too much trouble and I was following in his footsteps. I overheard Dad say that we didn't need such a big house. But Mom wanted a big house. We got the big house.

I don't mind the move. I stutter badly and fought a lot in Newmarket because kids made fun of my speech. Eric told me to fight any kid that makes fun of the way I speak.

Two weeks after we move, Mom and Dad give Eric and me "early Christmas presents." The gifts catch us by surprise. It's never happened before. I get a little white terrier and name him Shamus. Eric gets a drum set. I love my dog more than anything in the world and Eric treasures his drums.

Four days later, Eric and I arrive home from Montclair Middle Public School. We open the door to our nice big home. SMASH! Mom chucks a vase at Dad, barely missing his head.

"You're an asshole," she screams.

"Yeah, well you're a crazy bitch," Dad responds.

I gaze up at my brother in fright.

"It's okay. Let's go see Shamus," he says. We go to the backyard where Shamus slouches in the corner, his ears pinned back. I see sadness in my pooch's eyes. The shouts coming from inside the house have startled him. I pick up Shamus to comfort him and begin to cry. Eric sits with us.

"What's happening to Mom and Dad?" I ask.

"They hate each other," he says.

I lean back against the gold-coloured fence. I don't understand how Mom and Dad can hate each other.

"I'm going over to Rick's house," Eric says. "I'm not listening to this shit!"

I sit and scratch Shamus behind his ears. Shamus solemnly positions his head on my lap. Shouts erupt from the windows of Dad and Mom's bedroom. They yell at each other for more than an hour.

Dad approaches me with a worried, apologetic look on his face. "Where's your brother?"

"At Rick's." I try hard not to cry again. Eric told me that I'm weak if I cry.

"Are you okay, pal?" Dad asks.

I can't help it. Tears start to flow. "Why do you and Mom hate each other?"

"We don't hate each other, Shane. Sometimes parents just don't get along so well anymore. Come with me to get your brother."

"Why?"

"We all need to have a talk."

"I don't want to leave Shamus. He's sad. You guys scared him."

"I'm sorry, pal. Shamus can come."

We stay silent during the car ride back home. Eric sits in the back seat of the Ford Taurus and looks pissed off. Dad looks worried as he drives. I sit in the front seat. Shamus sits on my lap. He sticks his head out the window and enjoys the wind in his face.

When we get home, Mom is sitting in the living room.

"Go see your mother," Dad says.

I walk over to her. "Are you okay, Mom?"

"Sure, honey." She uses the sleeve of her purple blouse to wipe the tears from her face. "Everything will be alright."

Dad and Eric enter the living room and sit down on our new beige sofa. I huddle with Mom and Shamus on the loveseat. She places her arm around me and softly rubs the back of my neck.

"Kids, we need to talk," Dad says. "We're going to move again."

I look at him with tear-filled eyes and ask, "We're moving together, right?" I feel miserable, crushed, and worst of all, I know the answer.

"No son, we're not."

"Who am I going to live with? I'm n...nn...not picking. Please, ddd...don't make me pick," I shout.

"Don't worry, honey." Mom pulls me in close. "We'll figure all that out later. Your father and I want you boys to know that we will always love you and nothing will ever change that."

"Did I do something wrong?" I ask.

"This has nothing to do with anything either of you boys did," Dad replies. "Please don't ever think that."

Just like that, nineteen years of marriage ends. Dad and Mom continue their screaming matches for the month that it takes to sell the house.

~~~

I pack the last box in my Toronto Blue Jays-themed bedroom. Nothing remains except Shamus, who frolics with a tennis ball in the corner. Eric casually strolls into my room. He seems calm and undisturbed.

"I told you that you're stupid and that they're gonna get a divorce." Eric glares at me, shakes his head, and places the headset from his Sony Walkman over his ears. He turns and as he leaves my room, I hear Bon Jovi's "Bad Medicine" blare from his Walkman.

"So much for the perfect house," I mumble to myself.

Little Bird

Anna Li

I don't remember why Mom's yelling. I've stopped keeping track. Probably something I forgot to do. Dammit. Now I remember. I forgot to throw out the other half of my sandwich at lunchtime. My eyes fall to my lunch bag on the kitchen counter, zipped open like a gaping red mouth. The cellophane-wrapped half-sandwich lies inside, staring at me accusingly. *You knew this would happen. You should've just eaten me.*

I realize Mom is still yelling at me when she slaps my cheek with the back of her hand and I feel the air from the swing ring past my ears. Mom grips my arm and drags me down the hallway, her thick plastic slippers thwacking the hardwood floor. She rounds the corner of the bathroom, dragging me with her. The metal door latch catches my hip and tears my thin cotton shirt, grazing the skin underneath.

Mom hurls me to the floor. "You are a spoiled and ungrateful child. Think about what you have done."

Mom slams the door shut, rattling the mirror in the cabinet beside me. The lights remain off. The crack under the door lets in some light, so I can still see a little bit. The heating vent hums quietly. I can feel the chenille bath rug under my legs and nail clippings that missed the garbage can. I use the pads of my fingers to press onto the clippings and lift them into the bin. They prick my fingers.

The bathroom smells like burnt hair and Mom's cherry-blossom-scented shampoo. I don't move to turn on the lights. I curl my legs beneath me and hug myself. I will myself to remain still. I pretend my thighs are a piano keyboard and tap my fingers through the air, practising the sonatina I learned last week. I don't know what time it is. I don't know how long she wants me in here.

I hear dishes break, porcelain clattering on the ceramic floor in the kitchen. Water runs. She may be washing the dishes, but it sounds more like she's throwing the contents of the sink onto the floor.

I hear a squawk from the living room. One of Mom's coworkers gave us a canary last week as a gift. I named him Aden. He's not used to the noise yet. He's indignant, emitting little chirps of displeasure. I hear Mom stomp across the living room. She slams the cage to the floor. Birdseed scatters over the hardwood. Aden cries out and his wings beat the bars.

You'll have to get used to it, little bird. Just like the rest of us.

Silver Spoons

Mike Pitocco

I stare into the bathroom mirror and run my fingers through my hair. White flakes from the dried-out sport gel fall into the sink like snow in a blizzard. I splash cold water on my face, spritz Givenchy cologne on my collarbone and caress my freshly-shaven face.

I open the bathroom door and step into the hallway. My suitcase leans against the wall. I kneel down, pull open the zipper and rifle through the suitcase. I check to make sure that I have everything I need: five polo shirts, three pairs of jeans, a handful of socks, seven pairs of boxers, flannel pyjamas, a baseball cap and a collection of toiletries in a Ziploc bag.

I fasten the zippers and drag the suitcase down the stairs and into the kitchen. I set it on the marble counter. Mom and Dad watch me from the kitchen table. Mom taps her fingers.

I scramble down the staircase behind them into the basement before any of us can speak. To my right, seven guitars swing on hooks in the wall from their headstocks. I grab my black Taylor acoustic, throw it into a travelling bag, and race back up the stairs. My pace slows when I reach the kitchen.

"Are you ready to go?" Dad barks.

"Yes, Dad."

"You've got your wallet? Your phone? All your clothes are packed?"

"Yes, Dad."

"Are you sure?"

"Yes, Dad."

"You haven't forgotten anything?" He sneers. "You always forget something. Move!"

Dad gets up from his chair and rummages through my suitcase. Neatly folded clothes quickly become a tangled mess.

"Where is your deodorant? Your passport? Jesus, Mike! How many pairs of socks do you need?"

"The deodorant is in the Ziploc bag. My passport is in my pocket. I need seven pairs of socks, Dad. I'll be gone for a week."

He jerks the suitcase shut, yanking the zipper off its tracks. I hand him my guitar while I fix the zipper.

"What's the guitar for?"

"It's writing week, Dad. The other songwriters play piano and drums. I'm the only one who plays guitar."

"This isn't allowed on the plane! You'll have to check this with your luggage! I'm not paying for two pieces of baggage! Damn it, Mike. This one is coming out of your pocket!"

"Okay, Dad."

"This is so typical of you, trying to take advantage of us!"

"Sorry, Dad."

"You're damn lucky we're even letting you go!"

"I know, Dad."

His voice escalates. "And you better not lose this guitar! You're always losing things. It wasn't cheap, you know!"

"I know, Dad. I'm the one who bought it."

I fiddle with the zipper until the tracks realign and close the suitcase. I take back the guitar bag, sling it over my shoulder and grip the handle of the suitcase. "Alright, I'm going now."

Mom and Dad follow me as I walk towards the front door. Dad stops me. "Do you even know how to get to the airport?"

"Yes, Dad."

He sneers. "Yeah, right. Just be careful getting there! There's traffic this time of day!"

"Okay, Dad."

"And don't drive so fast, follow the speed limit! And for God's sake, don't play your music so loud, you'll kill somebody!"

"Okay, Dad."

"You've got the money I gave you?"

"Yes, Dad."

"You better be smart with it! I didn't give it to you to spend on drugs and hookers!"

"I know, Dad."

"And call home when you land in New York!"

"Okay, Dad."

"Don't forget! You always forget! Your mother will be worried sick—you know how she gets!"

"I know, Dad. I won't forget."

"Fine. Good. Give me your luggage. I'll put it in the car. It's probably too heavy for you. You're not that strong, you know."

"I'm fine, Dad."

"Fine. Get going. What are you still doing here? You're gonna make yourself late. For God's sake, tuck your shirt in, you look like a slob!"

"Okay, Dad."

I open the screen door and step onto the veranda.

"Wait," Dad yells. "Take the GPS! Here, I'll program the airport address in it. I don't want no phone call from you asking me to come get you when you get lost!" He hands me the GPS. "Here, take the car charger too. Did you even comb your hair?"

I shove the charger into my pocket and continue down the veranda.

"Bye," I shout, my back still facing them.

"Hey!" Dad scoffs. "Don't forget to call!"

I nod. He grunts and closes the door. The clunk from the deadbolt vibrates down the porch. I pivot and continue on down the driveway towards my car. I toss my luggage into the trunk of my Nissan Versa and balance the guitar across the backseat before I settle into the driver's seat. I thrust my key into the ignition and wait for the hum of the engine. "Blown Away" by Carrie Underwood screams at me through the radio.

I place the GPS into the empty cup holder, shift into reverse, and back out onto the empty road. I throw it into drive as the song reaches the bridge.

> *There's not enough rain in Oklahoma*
> *to wash the sins out of that house.*
> *There's not enough wind in Oklahoma*
> *to rip the nails out of the past."*

I accelerate towards the highway and steal a final glance at my house. Dad stands in the dining room. From the bay window, he watches as I drive away.

Grandfather

Simin Emadzadeh

I hold Grandpa's hand and Mom holds his other hand as we walk him to his room. His knee trembles with every step he takes. I feel the wrinkles on his hands. Loose skin hangs from his arms. He looks fragile. We hold him tight so that he doesn't fall.

My grandparents' apartment in Iran has three bedrooms and a living room with a long, narrow hallway that leads to the dining room. The kitchen opens to a TV room where the dinner table has been placed.

It takes us almost fifteen minutes to walk from the bathroom to Grandpa's bed. His eyes look tired and his hands feel cold. Mom dries droplets of sweat from his forehead with a towel and then kisses him. He looks at Mom's face with his big bug eyes.

"Where is Banoo?" he asks.

"Dad, she went to get your prescription," Mom says. "She will be home soon."

"Banoo," he calls out for Grandma, his eyes scanning the room.

"I just told you, Baba, she will be back very soon."

Grandpa looks up at Mom again, then looks away.

I take the towel back to the bathroom while Mom sets up Grandpa's diaper. She never lets me stay in the room when she changes his diaper. I return and see Mom, bent forward, holding her back with both hands. Pain lines her face. Mom always has back-aches, but still won't let me help her change Grandpa's diapers. I help Mom put his clothes on.

We lay Grandpa down on his bed. Mom massages his feet. The doctor said massage is the best way to help his blood circulation, since he can't walk much anymore. I put moisturizer on his dry feet and scrub them.

"Banoo...Banoo...Banoo," Grandpa shouts again and tries to hold his head up.

"Baba Bozorg, she's not home yet," I tell him.

"Where did she go?" he asks. "Why did she leave me?"

"She didn't leave you. She went to buy your medications. She will come back soon."

I rub his hand.

"I have to go finish cooking, Simin," Mom says and heads to the kitchen.

Grandpa looks agitated. His fragile arms and trembling shoulder can barely pull up his blanket. It hurts to watch. At one time, Grandpa was the most intimidating person I had ever known. Strict as a dictator, he never let anyone get away with a single breach of his rules. Everyone respected and feared him.

The weekends I spent at his house were fun only when he wasn't home. He wouldn't let us play and be loud. During meals, we had to sit at the dinner table and no one was allowed to leave without his permission—even when the phone rang. "Whoever it is, cut it soon and come back to the table," he would yell at Grandma.

Grandpa set a strict curfew for Mom, my brothers, my cousins and me. No one was allowed to come home later than eight at night. We all hated his strictness. It was torture for us to shut the lights at ten and stay quiet. His presence triggered tension and fear in all of us.

"Banoo," he shouts again.

"Baba Bozorg, she is on her way home."

Grandpa looks into my eyes. "Who are you?" he asks.

"I am your grandchild, Simin," I say in a soft voice.

He looks away. He pushes his sheet off the bed to the floor and tries to sit up. I pick up the sheet and sit him upright.

"Are you hungry, Baba Bozorg?" I ask. He traces the flower patterns on the sheet with his fingers and pushes it away again.

"Banoo," he calls. "Where is Banoo?"

Marketing

Dana Bibi

M s. Nawal rubs her right shoulder. The gesture seems subtle and delicate and at the same time frantic. I understand the signal. My allotted hour of presentation to the Jordanian Female Pioneers of Knowledge Club of Amman is over. The women's eyes glazed over ten minutes ago.

Finger foods lie arranged on a large glass table in Ms. Nawal's parlour. The enticing smell wafts around us.

I nod my head in Ms. Nawal's direction, take a deep breath, and conclude my fourth presentation of the week.

"Spirulina is a dietary supplement harvested from algae. My uncle's company grows it especially for you. If anyone is interested in ordering, please see me after. Thank you for your time."

All twenty-nine women titter and clap. My professional smile slides into a wide grin. Ms. Nawal shepherds her guests toward the finger-food spread. She clucks at the women. Her heels clack against the marble floor.

I turn around to collect my highlighted cue cards. I take five minutes to pack all the samples, brochures and stray business cards into my shiny briefcase and tuck the briefcase behind a plastic potted plant, beside delivery boxes from a local catering company. I slowly edge towards the refreshment table and the loud chatter, exaggerated laughter, obnoxious coughs and clinking cutlery.

A lady wrapped snugly in a bright red blazer notices me. She insists I try the homemade cinnamon rolls and the homemade cheese bread and the homemade rice pudding and the homemade chocolate mousse and the homemade fruit tarts.

She sniffs at me. "Dana, *habibti*, dear, how old are you? Only eighteen? You study at the University of Toronto, eh? Did you know that I have a son there? Yes, it's true, and he's in his fourth year, habibti."

Her words rush at me. I stop chewing. My eyes dart around the room. I do not want to have this conversation—not again.

Ms. Red Blazer, undaunted by my lack of response, puffs up. She fumbles for her iPhone, slides it out of her pocket and scrolls through the screen. "See, here is a photo of him in that Square Mall in Mississauga. He's studying to be a doctor. Just like his father. You like that, eh?"

I flash a tight smile at her proffered pictures. I wonder if he knows that his mother markets him this way. I wonder if they all know that their mothers market them this same way. I gesture that I need a napkin. I step away before she can block my exit.

My elbow sinks into something soft. Ms. Nawal screeches. I quickly pull away from my host's hip. "Dana, there you are! I've been looking all over for you!" She loads several crispy pastries onto my plate.

"What a wonderful home, Ms. Nawal. Thank you for the food and your—"

"Nonsense! It's so good that you are working this summer! We always wanted to have a smart, hardworking, pretty girl like you here. It gets so lonely in this mansion."

I try not to inhale through my nose. Her musky perfume overwhelms me. The scent clashes with the food's aroma. I set my plate down on the glass table between platters of fruit and tiramisu.

An argument breaks out between a woman in a pleather dress and her taller friend. They gesture wildly, pointing at the crystal light fixture above, the rose bouquets, the white curtains and the grand piano in the corner.

Squeaky sighs, jangling jewellery and a superior sniff brings me back to Ms. Nawal's large presence. She sweeps her hands through the air and they settle on my shoulders. She leans in close. Red lipstick stains her teeth.

"I want to tell you about my son." She coughs in a dainty manner.

I hurry to change the subject. "Oh no, Ms. Nawal. Do you cough often? Spirulina is what you need to relieve your respiratory system."

"Yes, yes, I know. You'll get your sale later. But see, my son, my boy, he is graduating this year from the University of Waterloo."

I struggle to suppress my groan.

Her eyebrow arches at my silence. "Take his number so you can meet and talk! He is a good boy, prays all the time, don't worry!"

She presses a thin sheet of paper into my right hand.

"No thank you, Ms. Nawal. He sounds like a nice person, but I'm not here for that."

Ms. Nawal purses her lips.

I take the opportunity to thank her graciously for allowing me to promote my uncle's product in her home. She clasps me to her heaving bosom. Her silver necklace snags my blouse as I pull away for air.

I feel a sharp tap on my shoulder. I turn around. A red fingernail poises in my face. "You have a gift for words. I have a son who studies law…"

I find my plate on the table in front of me. I hide my grimace behind a strawberry cupcake. I'm contracted to remain here for another hour. I chew slowly.

The Door

Rahul Sethi

A gale wind blew off the door of our basement apartment. As Mom carried in groceries, the strong wind drove her into the open door. The collision wrenched the door and hinges from the frame.

The Punjabi landlord didn't speak about the many flaws in the basement's apartment's design when my parents and aunt and uncle looked over the place before moving in. But as he stands outside with Mom and considers the door on the ground, the exposed entranceway to our apartment and the six-month rental agreement signed three weeks earlier, the landlord's tongue slips loose.

"*Everything* they did backward. You can't trust Punjabis to do a proper job." He shakes his head. "I should have got Italians."

The landlord counts out the positive traits of white folks by touching the tip of his thumb to the creases of his pinkie. "They're always professional. They do the job right the first time and they never complain about the work or how much they're getting paid. Our folk are a sneaky lot."

Mom nudges the door with her foot, like a child standing on a bed trying to rouse her little sister.

"And you know..." A cold wind sweeps over the landlord. He wraps his scarf tighter around his neck and shoves his hands under his armpits. "The idiots. When they laid the cement for this," he stomps his foot on the cement walkway that leads to the basement, "they made it slope toward the house. It hasn't happened this winter yet—and I hope it never happens—but it always happens that snow leaks through the walls onto the floor, wetting my carpet."

It's ten in the evening when Mom finally comes in from her talk with the landlord. He told her it was impossible to attach the door without replacing the doorframe. The wood that the hinges screw into had snapped into splinters and woodchips. The landlord said Mom would have to buy the new frame since she had fallen into the door. "The wind alone couldn't have blown it off," he said. "You should be more careful when walking."

It's too late to go to the hardware store. Aikenhead's at Warden and Eglinton closed at nine. Mom has to wait until tomorrow. Besides, Papa and Gulu Uncle drove the Honda Civic to work and won't be home until seven in the morning.

Every evening, Papa and Gulu Uncle head to the printing factory carrying their *tiffin* boxes, a steel lunchbox with four separate containers that latch together—one for rice, one for curry, one for roti and one for a sweet dish. They work the nightshift at a factory on Midland and Ellesmere, printing synthetic Nike, Reebok and Adidas logos on T-shirts, shorts and hats. Papa sometimes brings home Nike T-shirts and shorts for my brother Rohit and me. He brings home shirts that have a rip here or a tear there and can't be sent to the stores. The logos usually fade after a second wash.

Mom grabs a roll of Scotch tape from a drawer in the kitchen. She tells us to put on our coats, hats, gloves and extra pants and socks until she and Babita Aunty fix the door. We make breath clouds while we slide into the extra layers.

Babita Aunty wraps another blanket around baby Nitin and squeezes chubby little Nikita into woollen socks, a jacket and snow pants. She changes into winter clothes and climbs the flight of stairs to the entrance door. As she walks up, Babita Aunty rolls her long hair into a bun, pulls out a pen from her pocket and pokes it through her hair to hold the bun in place.

Wind gusts into the basement as Mom and Babita Aunty try to fit the door back into the frame. Mom lifts the door up from the ground and manoeuvres it to where it once stood in the entrance way. From inside the basement, she grips the doorknob to hold the metal door in place.

"Babita." Mom gestures to the doorknob. "Hold this."

Babita Aunty steadies the door as Mom runs the Scotch tape wall to wall and makes a web of tape to hold the door in the frame. Mom tells Babita Aunty to let go of the doorknob. A few moments later, the heavy door peels itself away from the web of tape and falls with a thud to the cement walkway outside. We all flinch. Mom crosses her arm over her waist and raises a fist to her lips. The door is too heavy for the tape to hold.

Mom and Babita Aunty rummage through the basement for any boxes and plastic bags they can find. Mom gives Rohit, little Nikita and me each a bowl of Count Chocula for dinner and adds the cereal box to the pile.

Mom and Babita Aunty take the pile of cereal boxes, Chiquita Banana cardboard boxes from grocery shopping at No Frills, empty Bata shoe boxes and garbage bags. They tape the collection into a collage the size of our entrance door. They take it up the stairs and cover the open entranceway. Mom runs the Scotch tape from wall to wall, making another web of tape.

The makeshift door flaps and rustles from the wind that billows in the walkway. It's light enough, and the tape holds. But after a few more gales of wind, the tape begins to give way. Another strong gust blows one side of the makeshift door off the wall, and it flaps like a flag in the wind.

Mom quickly grabs a few nails and thumbtacks from a drawer in the kitchen, picks up the hammer that sits in our shoe rack and runs to the entrance. She nails and thumbtacks the door to the walls and doorframe. She stands at the entrance for a few minutes, the hammer dangling from her thin hand.

The door rustles, but it holds.

We all sit on the couch in our small living room—me, Mom, Babita Aunty, Rohit and little Nikita. A portable heater stands in the middle of the living room, rotating and blowing heat. Baby Nitin lies asleep in his crib, wrapped in three blankets with a little toque on his head.

Mom puts on a video of *TaleSpin* episodes that Rohit recorded on the VCR. She takes off our jackets and extra layers and covers us with a blanket. We sit huddled on the couch and watch Baloo and Kit outwit Don Karnage. We all doze while dogs, tigers and hyenas fly propeller planes and seek to steal pricey cargo from a pilot bear and his sidekick cub. We sleep through the night on the couch.

Mom and Babita Aunty awake in the morning to see Papa and Gulu Uncle standing in front of us in the living room, loosely holding their tiffin boxes.

"What happened?" Papa gestures to the entrance with a nod. "What happened to the door? We had to tear that thing open to get inside."

Papa and Gulu Uncle have torn a wide gap in the centre of the door, large enough for them to fit through.

"Did you show the landlord?"

Mom gets out from under the blanket. Rohit, little Nikita and I look up. "Come," Mom says. She puts on her winter jacket and boots. She stretches out her hand and asks for the keys to the Honda Civic. "We have to go."

~~~

Two weeks after the door blew off, snow melts and the basement carpet soaks up a minor flood, drenching our socks when we walk.

The Visit

Mark Bialy

I sit on the couch in the family room and sip hot tea. My eyes watch *SportsCentre* on the TV but my mind wanders to what Grandpa will look like when he visits today. I'm fifteen years old and I've never seen my dad's father. Not even in pictures.

Grandpa lives in Toronto, where Dad grew up. I don't know much about Dad's side of the family. He has two brothers. His mother died before I was born and his father has lived alone ever since. If it wasn't for Mom nagging Dad to invite Grandpa over, I don't think I would be meeting him.

Dad, smelling of Ralph Lauren Polo cologne, grabs his wallet off the counter and the keys to the Mercedes-Benz. "I'll be back in a few hours." He rarely drives the Mercedes.

Two hours later, Dad calls on his cellphone and says they're almost home. My sister Amanda and I hustle upstairs to our rooms and change into our church clothes. I put on khaki pants, a white dress shirt and a blue argyle sweater.

Mom cooks meatloaf, mashed potatoes and cauliflower in the kitchen. "Amanda! Marek!" Mom shouts. "Can one of you set the table?"

I take five gold-rimmed plates out of the oak cabinet and set them down on the dining room table. I place silver cutlery around each plate—fork on the left, knife on the right, dessert spoon above. Amanda sets the napkins and glasses. I open the blinds.

The doorbell rings. Amanda and I stare at each other.

Mom opens the front door. "Why, hello there!" Mom says. "It's so good to finally meet you! I'm Peter's wife, Margaret."

I hear Mom and Grandpa exchange kisses.

"Yes, yes, Margaret. I am so glad to be here and see you," Grandpa replies. "You are so beautiful."

I look at Amanda and we inch out of the dining room. A slender man stands inside the door, about six inches shorter than Dad. He wears a baseball cap, leather jacket and loafers. Grandpa's small head, beady eyes and sharp nose contrast with Dad's big head, wideset eyes and round nose.

"*Dziadek!* Hi," I say.

I give Grandpa a hug. Amanda does the same. He squints and cranes his neck towards us. "My goodness, you kids are so tall! Marek, you look just like your father!"

"He gets that from everyone." Mom chuckles. "Come in, Tato. Make yourself at home. Dinner will be ready soon."

Dad hangs Grandpa's jacket in the closet and places his cap on the closet shelf. I lead Grandpa into the family room and we sit on the couch. Dad changes the TV channel to golf and sits on the single chair to our left.

"You know, Tat, Marek is doing well in school," Dad says.

Grandpa leans forward. "What's that?"

I notice a hearing aid in his ear.

"Marek is doing well in school," Dad says louder.

"Oh, that is great to hear." Grandpa looks at me and smiles. I smile back.

Grandpa turns his head and watches golf. He sits with his feet crossed and his hands between his thighs. His arched back doesn't touch the back of the couch. Dad fiddles with his thumbs.

"Do you like watching golf, Dziadek?" I ask.

"It's okay. I sometimes watch it at home."

The conversation ends there. I sit quietly beside Grandpa. Mom walks into the room. "Dinner is ready, everyone."

Dad and Grandpa take the heads of the table. Mom holds a camera. "Marek, Amanda, stand beside Dziadek and I'll take some pictures."

Amanda and I huddle around Grandpa. Dad smiles and his eyes glisten from across the table. Mom takes three pictures. "Perfect. Now let's eat!"

Grandpa tucks his napkin into the neck of his sweater and loads one slice of meatloaf, two spoons of mashed potatoes and a piece of cauliflower onto his plate. He leans his head over his plate and struggles to cut his meatloaf. Rough hands and bruised fingernails show the remnants of his days as a railroad mechanic.

Dad sits with his elbows on the table and scoffs down mashed potatoes. Grandpa chews with his head down.

"You know, Tato, Marek painted that picture of Pope John Paul behind me," Mom says.

Grandpa's head shoots up. "Wow. That is beautiful. When Peter was a little boy he always sat by the fridge and drew cartoons. He would—"

"Tat, nobody wants to hear about that," Dad mumbles through a mouthful of food.

Mom peers over at Dad. "Piotrek, of course we want to hear about it."

Amanda and I nod. Grandpa smiles. He looks at his food and swirls his mashed potatoes. Grandpa doesn't attempt to share any more memories.

He grabs a piece of cauliflower by the stem and eats it with his head down. Spots of gravy cover his napkin and a bit of cauliflower rests on the top corner of his lip. He finishes his meal and wipes his mouth with his napkin. He notices gravy smears on his chin and wipes them off with the palm of his hand.

"Would you like some dessert, Tato?" Mom asks. "I have cheesecake in the fridge."

"No thank you, Margaret. I should get going. I have things to do at home. Thank you so much for a great dinner and for inviting me to your home."

Grandpa pushes his seat back, stands up, then reaches into his pocket. He pulls out two cheques.

"Marek and Amanda, these are for you." He hands Amanda one cheque and me the other. Dad looks at the amount—$3,000. His eyes fill with tears.

"Tat, you don't have to do this. This is too much," he murmurs.

"No, no, those are for the kids," Grandpa says. "I have missed out on so much. This is the least I can do for them. Put the money in your bank accounts, kids."

"Thank you, Dziadek," I say and give him a long hug.

"Thanks, Dziadek," Amanda says and hugs him, too.

Grandpa walks to the front door and slips on his loafers. Dad pulls Grandpa's coat and baseball cap out of the closet and hands them to him. Grandpa zips up his coat, bends the brim of his cap and places it on his head. Mom, Amanda and I take turns hugging Grandpa. Dad grabs the keys to the Mercedes and opens the front door. Grandpa smiles, turns, and walks out.

"I'll be back in a few hours," Dad says.

Put a Hole in It, Won't You

Emily Davidson

The oven clock blinks 8:13. We have to leave by 8:30.

"Have you guys eaten yet?" Mom yells from upstairs, over the noise of her hairdryer.

"We're doing it right now," I screech from the kitchen.

Mom feels guilty leaving early. She teaches problem kids at Edenrose Public School. Mom stomps down the stairs and approves Eric's breakfast choice—Shreddies with sliced bananas and oatmeal crunch. She rolls her eyes at my mine—Lucky Charms. Mom buys Lucky Charms because she likes them, too.

Mom moves through the kitchen and family room as she pulls rollers from her hair. She leaves them scattered around the house.

"Have you guys seen my keys? Where are my car keys?" Mom barks at us in her get-a-move-on voice.

We transform into car-key searchers. A long ten minutes later, the keys reveal themselves—on the hook where they belong.

Mom pulls on her brown jacket. "At least be civil with each other," she tells us.

Yeah, right.

I sit next to Eric at the breakfast bar and spoon the last floating purple horseshoe marshmallow into my mouth. I study Eric's face. I hate his pointy nose. I hate his black clothes and I hate his voice. Eric reminds me of cold, clammy feet. His eating habits make me shudder.

"Why can't you just stop breathing?" I ask.

"Why can't you just spill Super Glue on your face?" Eric crunches a mouthful of Shreddies.

"You disgust me," I say.

I elbow Eric during the "cereal-eating moment of truth." The milk in Eric's spoon swishes. Some Shreddies make it to his mouth. The rest cascade onto his lap.

I point and giggle.

Eric's dark eyes examine the stain on his crotch, then look up and meet mine. I run. My long legs carry me swiftly up the stairs, but Eric stays at my heels. I slam the door to my room. Eric's fists pummel the other side. I lean hard against the door.

"Ha!" I say. "You're such a loser."

Eric pounds his fists as my muscles strain to hold the door shut. I hope he doesn't rip my horse posters taped to the outside of my door.

The clock beside my bed blinks 8:22.

Silence ripples through the hallway. My heart pounds in my ears. "If you think pretending to be gone is gonna make me come out, it won't!"

"Em," Eric says softly. "Come out. Promise you won't tell?"

"Yeah, right, dorkus. I'm not that stupid!"

"Seriously, Em. I won't hurt you. Just come out and see this."

I open the door slightly, on red-alert for a body slam. I squint one eye and peer through the tiny crack. Eric has his "oh-oh" face. I open the door. Eric points to a foot-sized hole in the centre of the door.

"Holy shit, dude. You are in so much trouble."

"Em, you can't tell Mom. Promise? Please?"

So this is what it feels like to play God.

"Look," I say. "I'll move this horse poster over the hole."

"Do you promise not to tell?"

"No, I won't tell. Pinky swear."

Eric and I peel the Scotch tape from the back of the horse calendar photos. We reposition all eight posters so that the new configuration looks natural.

At 8:45, Eric and I run to school.

~~~

Mom finds the hole in the door two years later.

Chapter 4: Relationships

Present a picture of a romantic
relationship by detailing events
you have experienced or observed.

Yellow

Andrew Ihamaki

The soles of my sneakers chirp against the tiled gym floor as I manoeuvre around Jessica's toes. Speakers blast the song "Yellow" by Coldplay from a mixed CD. Overhead streamers stir with the weight of everyone's hot breath. The basketball nets catch the lights from the strobe. Boys and girls stand separated at each end of the court, cradling the arcs of the three-point lines. Only Jessica and I, and three other couples, dance together.

The gym reeks of odour from the armpits of thirty twelve-year-old kids. Matt, Dan and Drew push and shove each other as they fight over who gets to dance with Jordan. Matt has Dan in a head-lock and Drew throws in a punch whenever he sees an opening. They have been fighting over the girl all night.

I rotate Jessica in tight, timid circles and study everyone and everything around us. I examine every brick on the wall, searching for a place to rest my eyes—anywhere but on Jessica. I settle on the wall over Jessica's right ear and follow the horizontal lines of the mortar until they reach the doorframe of the fire escape. I look down and smile awkwardly at Jessica, then nervously look back at the door.

Mrs. McCallum saunters past the bowl of lukewarm punch. She opens the fire escape door to alleviate some of the discomfort. The open door unveils a view of the sun setting over the hayfields outside. A soft breeze tickles the tips of Mrs. McCallum's short blonde hair. Her shawl catches flight, then drifts back to her shoulders. She grabs one of the vacant folding chairs that line the gym walls and props open the door. The outside air brings little relief.

Sweat seeps from my pores and beads slowly down my eyebrows and chin. My hands clam up as they hover over Jessica's waist. My stomach boils with nerves. My tongue goes numb. Words dribble out of my mouth like drool.

"You look so beautiful, Jessica," I say.

We lock eyes. She just smiles.

"No, Jessica, you're so pretty, like, definitely the prettiest ever." She smiles again.

I notice the clock on the wall from my skewed angle and see that its round standard face reads 9:15. The foul air in the gym still hangs heavy, but Jessica smells sweet. Her hair smells like vanilla. Her neck smells like cinnamon.

I move closer and work up the nerve to look at Jessica again. A single lock of her sandy blonde hair escapes her up-do. It falls and frames the left side of her face. Her skin glistens as we lock eyes again.

She smiles at me.

I love the way her smile makes her nose scrunch and squishes her freckles. My skin blisters with goosebumps. I want to kiss her so bad. I've had a crush on her since the first day of school. Now I tremble in a lake of cold sweat, unable to make the move and kiss Jessica.

The song continues to pump through the gym as we dance. The lyrics of "Yellow" mark each gut-wrenching second and say every word I wish I could. "You know I love you so. You know I love you so."

I lean in. I pull back. Any normal person would kiss her.

"Is everything okay?" she asks.

I swallow the bag of marbles in my throat and stare into her eyes. My heart runs laps as I work up the nerve to tell Jessica how I feel about her. I have so much to say. I want to tell her about the freckles on her nose, how she sometimes snorts when she laughs, and how I want to hold her hand every single day at recess. I want to tell Jessica all the things I love about her. I wish I could just rip the lyrics from the speakers and hand her a profession of my love.

Instead, as my feet barely miss crushing her toes, I whisper, "I mean it, Jessica. You are, like, so pretty. Really, like, so pretty."

She smiles.

Wen

Huamai Han

"W e must be careful," Nanfan tells his deskmate, Beihai. "My old classmate Li Wen got hepatitis."

I draw a *paowuxian* (parabola) for my grade-twelve math assignment. It is late February 1988 in our small northern Chinese city, Linyi.

"Oh." I turn to Nanfan and Beihai. They sit one row behind me. I feel awkward eavesdropping on their conversation, but I must ask. "Is he okay?"

"Well, he is staying in the hospital. I guess he is recovering." Nanfan, left hand still pressing his ruler, raises his head. Holding a pencil in his other hand, he pushes up his big glasses with his index finger and looks at me.

"Oh, good." I turn back and pretend to work on my math assignment.

In the self-study period before lunch break, I tighten my heavy cotton coat. Although a fire burns in the coal stove at the back of the classroom, the cold seeps into my bones. I stare out the green-framed window.

In the three rows of bungalows, my classroom sits in the middle of the first row. Wen's classroom hides behind a maple tree at the far corner of the second row. For the past two and half years, I've looked out the window and watched Wen walk toward the maple tree and out of my sight. Then I continue my reading. In the winter, the white mist on the window blocks my view. Every morning, I draw pictures with my finger on the glass. I have hardly seen Wen since school resumed after the Chinese New Year's holiday.

Hepatitis? Hospital? Sounds serious to me. Which hospital? How is he? Did he suffer? I have no idea. I don't want to ask.

———

Wen, my classmate since grade six, sits behind me in grade eight. Our home teacher, Mr. Li, suddenly finds a myth incarnate—that of a naughty boy becoming a good student—in Wen.

Wen looks like a grown-up, fit and strong. He has broad, thick shoulders. His black hair, nice and short, curls slightly—rare among Chinese people. He speaks in a cheerful tone with a beautiful voice. Wen often scratches his head with his right hand when he feels embarrassed or shy. When he smiles, the corners of his lips curve up and his eyes shine. He writes well with pen and brush, showing strong will, strength and beauty.

I anticipate Wen's arrival every morning. My heart races when he appears at the door. I stare down at my books and feel his shadow move across my desk. My back tenses during the day, with Wen right behind me.

In the early to mid-1980s, I attend Linyi Middle School Number One. I talk to boys, but I don't befriend them. "Talking love," as we call it, looks shameful. A few grade-twelve students have boyfriends or girlfriends, when all hope for attending university is lost. Mother expects me to continue high school at Middle School Number One. She expects me to pass university entrance exams. I can't be interested in Wen.

Two other girls in my grade-eight class like Wen. Yang Zi does not do well in school, but she is big and pretty. Lu Bing is not pretty, but she scores top three in our class. Their parents work for the Linyi Electricity Bureau. So does Wen's father. All three families live in the Electricity Bureau apartment building in Linyi. My family lives in the country. I stay in a school dorm and see my parents once every few months.

I often talk to the two boys who sit one row in front of me, Weidong and Guoqiang. They don't have much hope of staying at Middle School Number One after grade eight. Sometimes Nanfan comes and talks to Wen; sometimes Nanfan comes and talks to Weidong and Guoqiang; and sometimes Nanfan talks to me when I don't expect it. I respond to Nanfan. I hardly speak to Wen.

I spend all my waking time in the classroom. I stare at books and my mind wanders. I dream that Wen and I have a warm home in an apartment building in Linyi. Wen kisses me goodbye before we go to work. We run on the beach in early spring along the Yi River. Wen and I have a daughter and we watch her grow up.

My grades fly up and down like a kite. I hate myself when I get my exams back. I promise myself I'll concentrate. But I dream all the time.

I pass the entrance exams and enter grade nine at Linyi Middle School Number One. So do Wen, Nanfan and Lu Bing. Yang Zi, Weidong and Guoqiang move to other schools. There are eight grade-nine classes. Wen and Lu Bing go to class two. Nanfan and I go to class five.

Watching Wen pass by the window becomes part of my morning routine during my high school years. I believe Wen knows it. He often scratches his head with his right hand when he passes by.

One spring day, Wen passes my window and then turns around. His eyes catch mine. My heart jumps to my throat. I blush, turn, and fix my eyes on my books. I peek to the side after a long wait. Wen flings his brown bag over his right shoulder and walks toward the maple tree. He walks in a rhythm, sprinting and bouncing. I close my eyes. I see Wen smiling under the maple tree. I smile. I smile for a few days.

~~~

One week after Nanfan broke the news of Wen's hepatitis, I chat with Nanfan. "I heard that hepatitis develops either slowly or very quickly. The slower it develops, the harder to cure. What is Li Wen's situation?"

"His syndrome developed very quickly. He should be fine. But this is not good timing."

"It's sure not. Only three months left before the university entrance exams."

"Poor Li Wen," Nanfan says. "I hope he can get out of there very soon."

"Do you know how long he will stay there? It must be very frustrating and boring."

"Yeah, I think so." Nanfan lengthens each of his words. "I'm thinking of asking if some of our old classmates would like to visit him. Will you go with me?"

"Um, sure." I look at Nanfan. "Why not? He is our old classmate."

A few days later, Nanfan pokes me in the back with his pen. "Hey, Beihai and Changjiang want to visit Li Wen as well. What about this afternoon?"

"This afternoon?" I turn to Nanfan. "Uh, fine with me. Shall we go after school?"

"We can skip the last period. Night falls early and it is slippery outside. I'll tell Teacher Wang."

"That will be great."

I turn back to continue my English exercise. A minute later, I look down at myself. Changing clothes during the day will attract the attention of others. I'm wearing the mauve jacket I got for the Chinese New Year. The gentle colour looks warm and bright in the winter. I like the butterfly-shaped buttons. I rush to finish my assignment.

During lunch break, I run back to my dorm to fetch my favourite big scarf, with red, white and black stripes. I also collect a pair of mittens. I tuck them both in my desk drawer.

Nanfan pokes my back with his pen when Teacher Wang strolls out of the classroom. "Are you ready?"

"One second." I sweep everything on the desktop into my drawer. I lock the desk and walk to the door. I stop halfway. I go back, unlock my desk, and pull out my scarf and mittens.

Four of us bike to the hospital in the west part of the city. Nanfan, Beihai and Changjiang talk about school. I do not hear much. I focus on riding my bike on the icy road. We arrive and park our bikes by a long, narrow hut.

"Should be this way." Nanfan leads us eastward. A thin layer of ice covers the road. I slip. I tiptoe along the edge of the road.

"Hey, you guys," someone shouts. I recognize the cheerful voice. I stop and raise my eyes. Wen, wearing a long, heavy coat, stands hands in pockets, a few metres away.

"Hey, Li Wen. How are you? We are here to see you!"

I don't know if it's Nanfan, Beihai or Changjiang speaking.

All three boys walk towards Wen. They punch him on his shoulders. I move slowly to the middle of the road. I don't want to fall now, not now. I stand behind the boys.

"I am fine. But they won't let me leave." Wen scratches his head with his right hand and smiles at me. I smile back. His face looks yellowish. His chin has grown sharper. I lower my eyes and look at the ice in front of my feet.

"Where are you going?" asks one of the boys. "Can you leave the ward?"

Keep asking, please.

"I just sneaked out for a walk. Other people lie in bed all day. I get bored. I'm fine now, but they won't allow me to go home."

I listen to Wen's every word. We walk him to his ward. He insists that we not go in. We must be careful not to catch hepatitis before our university entrance exams. The boys chat in the cold for a few more minutes. I think about suggesting to Wen that he go inside; he might feel the late afternoon cold.

I finally say, "You've been out for a while. Will they look for you?"

I speak to Wen directly for the first time.

"No problem. They have gotten used to it." Wen curves the corners of his lips and little sparkles light up in his eyes. They all laugh. I blush and look away.

Nanfan, Beihai and Changjiang make Wen go back inside. They punch each other on the shoulders to say goodbye.

"Take care."

I speak to Wen for the second time.

"Thanks for coming." Wen smiles and scratches his head with his right hand.

We walk toward our bikes. I turn and look back.

Wen stands in front of the ward and smiles. He has his left hand in his pocket and scratches his head with his right hand. I smile back and wave.

~~~

In May, Nanfan tells me that Wen was finally released from the hospital and had visited the school. I was not there when he came.

I return to the country after writing the university entrance exams. I stay for the entire summer. One day around noon, I return from farming, with muddy feet. Nanfan and his bike stand outside of our yard. My country neighbours stare at us when I unlock the front door to let Nanfan in. In my seven years of studying in Linyi, Nanfan is the only one to visit me in the country during the summer.

August 1988, I travel to Linyi to pick up my admission letter to East China Normal University. Eleven of my classmates will be attending universities in Beijing and Ji'nan, the provincial capital of Shandong. In September, I make my way to Shanghai. The trip takes six hours on a slow train then another thirteen hours on a fast train.

The university campus is huge and beautiful, with trees, bushes, flowers, wide avenues, winding paths and a combination of classic and modern buildings. The river that cuts through the campus has a romantic name, River of Liwalida. Everything is more expensive than in Linyi.

My new classmates come from all parts of China, mostly from big cities. We speak Mandarin on campus. Shanghai people speak a dialect I don't understand. But it doesn't take long for me to figure out that *xiangwunin* means country bumpkins—a common word that Shanghai residents toss at people from the rest of China. I never learn to speak the Shanghai dialect.

Nanfan writes me letters from his university in Shandong. It feels good to have a connection with my past. I write to Nanfan about my university and Shanghai.

On New Year's Day 1989, Wen sends me a postcard. How does he know I am in Shanghai? How did he get my address? On the light blue postcard, an angel catches stars with a net and flies toward the moon. On the back, Wen writes in beautiful calligraphy:

> *We are chasing our dreams all the time, aren't we?*
> *Wish you a Happy New Year.*
> *Li Wen, Grade Twelve, Linyi Middle School Number One.*

I look at his handwriting and in my mind I see Wen smiling in front of the ward, left hand in his pocket, right hand scratching his head.

I go back to Linyi for the Chinese New Year's holiday. I enjoy the time with my family in our village Jiantou. I visit my best friend Hiayan in Linyi. It takes two hours by bike. We visit our teachers. We do not bump into old classmates.

In spring 1989, Nanfan addresses me as *Xue* in his letter. In northern China, we always use a person's full name. We omit family names of close friends. When people are deeply in love, some address their loved ones with single-syllable names. I write to Nanfan and address him with his full name. I tell him I have lots of school work and that I may not be able to respond to his letters promptly.

In May 1989, I join the university students' parade in Shanghai to show condolence to Mr. Hu Yaobang, the late general secretary of the Communist Party of China. Later, students all over the country demand that the Central Chinese Government promote democracy and fight against corruption. In Shanghai, we march and protest to show support for the Tiananmen Square hunger strike. One night, we hear that the Central Government is sending the army to Shanghai. We march in the rain, run, march more, and run again for nine straight hours. We want to prevent the army from entering Shanghai. I wonder what Wen is doing in Linyi. The army does not show up. We return to the campus. We walk through the main entrance and shout out, "We are back, *Hua Shi Da* (East China Normal University). We are back, Hua Shi Da." Many voices ring out. The main avenue of Hua Shi Da and the trees mix into a vague green through my tears.

The Student Association of Shanghai Universities decides on an "empty the campus" move. On June 2, I return to Jiantou. The evening of June 4, my parents and I listen to the radio. The People's Liberation Army of China drive tanks, carry guns, and march to Tiananmen Square. Father and Mother straighten their bodies in their armchairs. Their fingers, grabbing the armrests tight, turn white. They look at each other with wide eyes and then turn to me. Mother's lips tremble as she murmurs, "*Zhen mei xiangdao, zhen mei xiangdao* (This never occurred to me, this never occurred to me)."

I slide to the cold cement floor and cry.

Father sighs and stands up. He paces in the living room, hands folded behind his back. For the first time, Father looks stooped. Mother slides down beside me on the floor and rubs my back softly. "Thank good heaven, you are here—thank good heaven."

The university entrance exams continue on July 7. I don't know if Wen will pass this time.

In the fall of 1989, universities require faculty and students to report on their doings and thoughts during the previous summer. Gathering for political study becomes a weekly routine and requires attendance signatures. Wen writes to me. He attends Shandong

Electrical College in Ji'nan. I write back. Wen writes about his trips, about Linyi classmates' gatherings, about Ji'nan. I write about my new campus, classmates, professors, books and Shanghai. I count the days waiting for Wen's letters. I become quiet and check the mailbox three or four times a day when his letters arrive late.

In the summer of 1990, the Central Chinese Government enforces a one-month military training program for university students. Wen writes to me. He offers to pick me up at the Linyi train station. Haiyan offers to host me at her home.

I get off the slow train. Hundreds of heads gather on the platform. I see Wen. He wears a white T-shirt and stands in the first row outside the entrance. I walk towards him. Wen's shining eyes catch mine. His lips curve upwards and his right hand scratches his head. Haiyan sees me. She pushes herself forward in the crowd, waving and shouting. Many people push, shout and wave and force me out of the exit. I meet Wen and Haiyan and introduce them to each other. We push through the crowd. Haiyan bikes my luggage. Wen bikes me.

I sit behind Wen's broad back, look at the trees running backward and feel the soft summer breeze. Haiyan's home is only a fifteen-minute bike ride from the train station.

During the summer of 1991, Wen, the only son in his family, goes back to Linyi to work for the Linyi Electricity Bureau. I knew this would happen from the time he sat behind me in grade eight. Wen continues to write to me. He never asks me what I plan to do after graduation. He never asks me to go back to Linyi after graduation. He never writes the word "love." He never writes the word "like." Nor do I.

I wonder if I can find a job as a college instructor in Linyi. Mother and Father live in the country and have little influence in Linyi. I prepare for the entrance exams to graduate school. In 1991, I stay in Shanghai during the Chinese New Year's holiday. It is the coldest winter in my four years of university in Shanghai. The cold sucks my bones.

In late spring of 1992, Wen writes me a letter. His aunt has introduced a girlfriend to him. She graduated from university two years before and works in the Commercial Bank in Linyi. She is the daughter of Principal Ding at Linyi Middle School Number One. I have never seen this girl. But I like Principal Ding. He taught Wen and me math in junior high. It is a good match for Wen.

I cry. The first time I love someone, I love Wen for eight years. We never held each other's hand.

I write to Wen.

"Eight years later, finally, I can tell you I loved you."

~~~

In the fall of 1992, I start graduate school in Shanghai.

I never see Wen again.

Christine

Adam Giles

I turn onto Christine's street and roll towards her house. I see her white car in the driveway. I park on the road. I pick up the card and roses from the backseat. I hold them and stare at the steering wheel for a moment. I place the roses gently on the passenger seat. I open the door and step out of my car. I walk slowly to the front door. I stand, take a deep breath, and ring the bell. I wait.

Christine's brother answers the door—he looks surprised to see me.

"Hey. Is Christine home?"

"Yeah, just a minute." He turns around. "Christine!"

I look back at my car. My hands shake. Christine walks to the door wearing a white T-shirt and plaid pyjama pants. She furrows her eyebrows and curls her top lip.

"Hey," she says.

"Hey. Can I talk to you?"

Christine looks side to side and then back to me. "Uh, I guess. What are you doing here?"

"Can you come outside?"

"What's going on?" She steps onto the porch and closes the door. "We have company over right now. I can't talk too long."

"Okay. Please don't be shocked. But I came here to give you this."

I hand her the card. I pause. I look at the ground.

"And to tell you that I love you."

I can't lift my heavy head. I stare at the porch's grey concrete. I force my head up and look at Christine's face. I've never seen so much of the whites of her eyes before. Her lashes flicker up and down and her mouth remains open. I look at her mouth and wait for words to come out.

I wait and wait and wait. Silence.

"Okay," she mutters. "When did this happen?"

"It's been a while, but I never had the guts to tell you."

"So you just show up here, unannounced, and throw this on me while we have company?"

"I'm sorry but I just had to tell you now. I couldn't take it anymore. I know you're going back up to Lindsay tomorrow and I had to tell you face to face."

Christine fires a blank stare at me. I swallow some saliva.

"I brought something for you. It's in my car."

"I don't know, Adam," she says. "I should be getting back in now."

"Please," I say. "Just come over here."

I lead her to my car. I open the passenger door. I pick up the roses, turn around, and hand them to Christine. "Here."

Her eyes widen, squint, then open again. She holds out the card. "No. I can't take these."

"Yes, you can," I say quietly. "Please. Just take them."

"No!" she whines. "I've got company inside. They can't be seeing me walk in with flowers."

"So just hide them."

"No. Here." She holds out the card.

"At least take the card. You can hide that easily."

"Okay," she snaps.

"I hope you understand that I needed to tell you and I want to stay friends, no matter what, Christine."

"Okay." She nods. "I'll send you an e-mail or something when I get back to Lindsay."

I nod.

Christine runs back into the house. I walk around to the driver's side and open the door. I fling the roses onto the passenger seat, sit down, and slam the door. I speed away. Tears blur my sight. I turn onto Credit Valley Road and pass the Petro-Canada gas station. As I turn onto The Chase, I grab the roses off the passenger seat and throw them out the window.

I'm almost home when I shake my head and turn around at Sandown Road. I drive back to Petro-Canada to buy cigarettes. I don't know which brand to ask for since I've never bought a pack before—I've always just taken some from Dad's open packs around the house when I felt like smoking. I ask the guy behind the counter for the du Maurier's in the grey package—Dad's brand.

The guy turns around and looks at me. "The Special Milds?"

"Yeah, I think so." I look at the floor.

"Can I see some ID?"

I look up at him and squint. I fumble though my wallet and show him my driver's licence.

"King size?" he asks.

"Yeah."

"$4.73, please."

I hand him a five-dollar bill and he hands me some coins. I grab the pack of cigarettes and walk back to my car. I drive to Erin Mills Town Centre, turn into the parking lot, and look over a sea of open asphalt. Not one car in the lot. I pull into a spot and jam the gear selector into park. I turn the key backwards so that the engine's turned off and I can still listen to music. I listen to "Push" by Matchbox 20.

I wanna push you around
Well I will, well I will
I wanna push you down
Well I will, well I will
I wanna take you for granted
Yeah, yeah, yeah.

I rip the plastic wrapper off the cigarette pack, open it, pull out the silver foil and take out a cigarette. I place it between my lips and then fumble for an old lighter in the glove compartment. I light up. I look across the empty parking lot. Dim orange lights shine down on the grid of yellow lines painted over the black asphalt. I breathe in some smoke and blow it out the window. I pool the saliva in my mouth, curl my tongue, and spit out the window. I look over the city lights, at the cars driving along Erin Mills Parkway, at the empty parking lot. I smoke.

Sneaking Out

Juliver Ramirez

I hold my breath and listen for any signs of stirring within the house. I wait for five seconds. I hear nothing. I glance at the digital alarm clock—1:15 a.m. By now, everyone should be asleep. I can't wait around and confirm it, though. Kimberly is waiting for me.

I slink out of bed. I avoid turning on any lights. I arrange pillows to make it look like it's me under the covers. Even in the darkness, the decoy sucks. But it will have to do. I'll be back soon anyways.

I strip off my wife beater and shorts. My hands pat through the drawers of my dresser for my black jogging pants. I pull my navy blue hoodie from its hanger in the closet. I weave past the furniture in my room and locate the night table. I pocket the essentials—cellphone, keys—and ponder bringing my wallet. I feel like taking it with me, but debit and health cards during this venture would only be a hassle. I leave the wallet behind. I'll be fine. I'm only going to be out for an hour or so. No one will even know.

I take a last look at the digital alarm clock from the doorway—1:19 a.m. I slowly and carefully close and lock my door.

I take the lightest steps possible down the hall. The floorboards still creak. I bite my lip and pace myself as I go down the stairs. I don't even try leaving through the front door. Instead, I pick up my shoes from the door mat and tiptoe to the kitchen. The sliding door makes far less noise than the front door. Still, I handle the lock with both hands. I want to muffle and absorb the clicking. I'm not free yet.

Crickets chirp in the backyard. My neighbours' houses seem lifeless without lights. Somehow, the darkness out here is not as scary as the darkness in my house.

The windows of my parents' room stand open above me. I can't run off just yet. I tiptoe across the wooden porch with my socks on. I reach the grass and put on my shoes. I scale the fence, break into a jog a street away from home, and check over my shoulder. I smile.

I can make it to Kimberly's house, a thirty-minute walk, in twenty minutes by running. I text her updates every couple of minutes. She wants to know that I'm safe. But she also wants me to risk my life just to see her tonight.

When she texted me, "I need to see you tonight," I knew I had to do something to get her back. Our summer romance had turned sour.

I slow to a brisk walk when I see Kimberly's house. I wipe the sweat off my face with my sleeve. I lower my head to each of my armpits. I'm not surprised they smell, but I'm still annoyed. This meeting is supposed to be perfect.

I wait on Kimberly's driveway and try to slow my breathing. I text, "Hey, I'm outside."

A minute later, Kimberly strolls out. The security alarm beeps twice. The door closes with a thud. I grimace.

I walk up and hug her. Kimberly's hoodie smells just like her freshly-showered hair. I inhale her scent before she breaks from the hug. We sit side by side on her front steps and talk for two hours. We don't say anything meaningful. Kimberly hides her hands in her sleeves and blows into them for warmth. I put my arm around her to keep her warm. She shrugs it off.

Kimberly scrolls through Twitter and her text messages for most of the time. I just sit. I can't think of anything to say. A few raindrops dot the walkway. We climb into her mom's SUV because we can't go inside the house. The leather squeaks as we settle into the backseat. The silence contains us.

I finally spill out my thoughts. I tell her I don't want to lose her. I tell her my parents will get used to the idea of us, to just give them some more time. I tell her that I'm still trying. My voice quivers.

Kimberly stays quiet. She shakes her head and looks out the window. We sit for another hour.

"Look at me," I tell her. Kimberly's eyes look tired and sad. "Say something, please."

"Jules, I can't do this anymore. I get to see everyone whenever I want—Johnny, Martyna, Eunice. I can call them up at two in the morning and they would come out and chill with me. I can do that with everyone—everyone except my own boyfriend. What is that? Like, seriously. I can't do this."

The sky greys outside. It's five-thirty a.m.

Tears well in my eyes. I don't meet Kimberly's gaze.

"Alright, good night," I mutter. I pull on the door handle and start towards home.

"Juliver!" Kimberly calls after me. "Stop. Please, just stop!"

I keep walking. Kimberly catches up to me and pulls at my arm. "I won't let you walk home like this. I'm giving you a ride. Come on."

I don't want to look at her. I don't move. I wipe my tears with my sleeve so I can look into her eyes. Just for a moment. "I'm okay, really," I tell her.

A morning jogger stares as he passes by.

The raindrops on the passenger side window transfix me. We stay quiet the whole ride home.

The Birthday

Samantha Ashenhurst

wake up fully clothed. My head throbs. The taste of Smirnoff Ice
and pepperoni pizza coats my dry mouth. The sun shines in my
eyes through the slats of the white venetian blinds. I drag my sore
body to the edge of my bed and stand up on shaky legs.

The clock reads nine a.m. It's official—my teenage years have
come to an end.

I open my bedroom door a crack and listen to the house. Silence.
The pressure on my bladder forces me to the washroom across the
hall. I puke twice, relieving last night's party with every retch. I
scrub my grainy teeth until they feel smooth and new. The mirror
reflects my tired, makeup-stained face. I rinse my skin with cold
water and choke down three Tylenol tablets.

I leave the washroom. I look at my sister Shawna's closed bedroom door. She's still asleep. The carpeted stairs groan softly as I
descend to the main landing.

A scribbled note waits for me in the kitchen.

Happy birthday!
Went to Aunt Gwen's. See you this afternoon.
Xo Mom and Dad.

Bottles and plastic cups litter the kitchen counter. I ignore them
and pour a large glass of orange juice. I swallow the drink in five
large gulps. My throat is raw from smoking too much weed last
night and the juice soothes and burns.

I leave the empty glass in the already-full sink and sneak quietly down to the basement. Dark wood panelling covers the walls. The decrepit green carpet makes the room smell musty and stale. I find Mark asleep on our ratty, grey loveseat. His cropped, greasy black hair sticks up in all directions. His mouth lets out a gentle snore. I muffle a giggle as I observe Mark's skinny body sprawled on the loveseat. One of his bony arms lies across his chest, the other swings a few inches above the carpet. He wears a Melt Banana T-shirt and a pair of black shorts. The blanket tangles between his long, bare legs. His socked feet dangle over the edge of the loveseat.

I approach him quietly, intending to wake him with a kiss, then pause. Mark's white Nokia cellphone rests on the carpet next to the couch. A small light in the upper right hand corner flashes blue, indicating an unread text message. I step away from his dozing body and wonder who sent him a message this early on a Sunday.

My body trembles when I realize I already know the answer.

My feet feel hot in my new moccasin slippers, a birthday gift from Mark. I stand in the dark basement rec room, quietly biting the polish off my fingernails. Mark still snores. My eyes dart from his face to his cellphone. I decide I need to know the truth.

I snatch up his phone and sit cross-legged on the floor next to the couch. Mark's eyes remain closed. He doesn't stir. I unlock his phone. One unread message. I exhale heavily and inhale sharply. His phone shakes in my trembling hands. I study his face and determine that he's definitely asleep. Opening his inbox, I check the message's sender.

Vicki.

Of course.

Vicki, Mark's new coworker, who is such "a cool girl." Vicki, the one who Mark's gone out for drinks with most nights for the past month. Vicki, the one who just broke up with her long-term boyfriend. Vicki, the one who Mark hasn't yet let me meet.

The blue light blinks. My finger hovers over the Open button. I hesitate. Do I want to ruin my birthday. I look at Mark's sleeping form on the sofa next to me and reflect on the past three years. I remember, vaguely, when we used to talk about our future together. After a trip to Montreal last summer, we spoke of starting a life in a foreign city or travelling around Europe after my graduation. I'm not sure when or why those conversations stopped.

Lately, unanswered phone calls and ignored text messages have worried me, but Mark always has seemingly legitimate excuses. I try to recall if he offered an explanation for being three hours late to the party last night, but I don't think I even bothered to ask. I wasn't interested in starting a fight in front of my friends.

He sleeps. I bite my short nails.

I open Vicki's message.

"Can I have you tonight?"

My face flushes and my eyes water. I clutch Mark's phone in my hand and grit my teeth. I can feel my heart beat faster. I struggle to steady my breathing.

I sit on the carpet. I reread Vicki's words. I consider replying to her, to ask if she knows about me at all, but decide against it. I study the message until the words blur together and lose all meaning.

I stand above my sleeping boyfriend and toss his phone, message open, at his chest. It lands on his rib cage and jolts him awake.

"I think you've gotta go."

Mark looks confused. He picks up his phone and studies the screen. His eyes widen as he stares at the text message.

"She's just kidding around," he sputters.

Mark tries to stand up but the blanket, still wrapped around his legs, causes him to stumble. "This isn't anything."

"I think you've gotta go," I say again. My palms sweat and my body shakes. My face feels hot. I stand at arm's length from him, hugging myself. "We can talk later, I really don't care. But right now, you have to go."

Mark nods, his face blank. He throws a pair of black jeans over his shorts and grabs his black backpack. I walk him upstairs to the front porch, not bothering to remove my moccasins. A mourning dove coos in the distance as we stand and face each other. The sky is clear and blue. Across the street, Mr. Carson mows his lawn. My nose tickles and my eyes water at the smell of fresh-cut grass.

Mark hugs me, his thin arms wrapped loosely around my shoulders. I let him, but leave my arms and hands dangling defiantly by my sides.

"Call me later," he says into my hair. "I mean, call me when you want to talk. This isn't what it looks like. I mean it." He pulls away and looks into my eyes. "Happy birthday."

Mark shuffles across the street to the bus stop, fumbling in his pocket for the fare. I walk back into the house and lock the door behind me. I yank off my moccasins and whip them into the front hall closet. I place my fingers on my throbbing temples and head to the kitchen. I grab an oversized garbage bag from under the sink and start cleaning.

Mi Kyeong

Jason Swetnam

I work long days teaching a range of subjects at the Naeja English Academy in Chunchon, South Korea—vocabulary for kids with dried squid breath, conversation for earnest businessmen in three-piece suits, grammar for undergrads with stuffed animals dangling from their backpacks and literature for Korean housewives.

On my first day, when I saw "housewives" on the timetable, I expected *ajummas* wearing nylon windbreakers and tight perms with thermoses of tea and tin lunchboxes of kimchi and rice. What I found were beautiful, educated, neglected women with time on their hands.

Two weeks into the class, a new housewife shows up. She comes in late and we all stop talking. She introduces herself. Her name is Mi Kyeong. She does not have nor want an English name. She is forty, married to a French professor, has a sixteen-year-old daughter, holds an English Literature degree, and wears tumbled stone necklaces that dip into the wells of her collarbones. With an hour of class remaining, we all try to get resettled, but I notice that I find myself often talking only to Mi Kyeong. The other housewives shift in their seats. Some cough and some raise their hands. They ask about Heathcliff or Mr. Rochester. But Mi Kyeong and I keep talking about Hemingway.

"I love how there is no cause and effect with Hemmingway. It is all and and and," she says.

"Me too! I love that, too."

"Bullfights and wars and well-lit rooms."

"You've summed up Hemmingway."

The class ends. The housewives go home. I order *kal-guk-soo* (noodle soup with beef and dumplings). The restaurant driver delivers the food to my school on a moped. When I finish eating, I leave the ceramic bowl and metal chopsticks outside the door to be picked up later.

I have time to kill before my next class on CNN News. Students watch the previous night's newscast in English and copy it down, word for word. I have a foot pedal that rewinds the show. I preview the news for tonight's class. When it is done, my foot hits the pedal to rewind it, and I think about Mi Kyeong. My foot hits the pedal again and I think about Mi Kyeong.

Four weeks into the class, after the other housewives have left and we are alone, Mi Kyeong tells me that she thinks about me. A crate of apple pears arrives at my apartment on a Saturday morning with no note, but I know it's from Mi Kyeong.

She calls me on the phone and we meet in the evening and she drives me around Chunchon. This becomes a routine and each time the drive gets longer and farther from town. One night, we find ourselves in a hotel bar off the highway between Chunchon and Seoul, drinking and watching the lights on the river. We look at each other.

"Do you want to get a room?" I say.

"Yes!" she says.

Six months into the class, this extracurricular activity becomes unfun. Her kisses need too much of me. I ask too many questions about her husband. She gets careless with her excuses to him. Mi Kyeong figures out that I am no longer into the relationship. She doesn't show up to class. The third time this happens, with ten minutes left, my boss, Mr. Cho, leans through the doorframe with a concerned look.

"There is a phone call for you," he says.

I walk out of the room, make my way to the main office, and pick up the phone.

"I need to see you."

"This isn't a good time."

"I need to see you."

"Okay. Tonight."

Mi Kyeong's car waits outside my building. The exhaust fumes rise and mix with the red taillights and rain and it looks like a movie set for a clichéd story about a breakup. The headlights of the car shine down on the ground. I get in but we don't go anywhere. We sit and wait for the other to speak.

"What are you thinking about?" she asks.

"What are you thinking about?"

"I asked you first."

"Nothing. You?"

"I don't know. Think about me!"

"I can't."

"Why?"

"I don't know."

"Speak."

"I can't."

"Why?"

"I'm not a dog."

"Be more specific."

"Woof."

"Is that funny?"

"Woof."

"Why are you so quiet?"

"Why are you? We're both quiet. Why? Many reasons."

"Like what?"

"I don't know."

"Will you remember me?"

"Yes."

"Yes?"

"Yes, I will. Of course. What do you think? Do you think I'm the type of person who would forget?"

"No, I don't think so."

Silence. I think about my first real girlfriend and what I am teaching tomorrow and how hungry I am and my roommate at home and whether this anticipated kiss is going to be too big.

"I'll drive you closer to your door. It's so wet," Mi Kyeong says.

"You don't have to."

"Thank you. I will always remember you."

"I will, too. I hope you can be happy with your husband. He sounds like a good man."

I shake her hand and hold it and then come the lips. We kiss goodbye. I step out of the car into the rain and walk away from the glowing taillights.

Wish

Jayson San Miguel

I perch on the leather couch in the student office. I lean forward and clasp the edges of a square paper. My once soft, smooth hands feel rough and grainy. They tremble as I turn one pointed edge of the sheet over the other. I crinkle and crease the imaginary lines on the paper. With a break comes the beak, and with a twist, the tail.

Micky walks in to finish her shift at the exam undergrad office.

"You're still at it?" she says.

"That's 972 cranes. I think it's 972. I hope I didn't lose count."

"You think she's gonna count?"

"I don't know. Maybe. I just don't want to be short, you know."

I place my latest purple paper crane on the table with the others. An array of rainbow colours of origami paper, construction paper, newspaper, lined paper, napkins and old exams cut into little squares lie scattered on the table.

"Your hands must be numb by now."

"It's not that bad. Although, I'm probably gonna get carpal tunnel soon."

Micky laughs.

"You must really like her."

"Yeah, I guess so."

I rummage through my stuffed backpack. My fingers graze over notebooks, textbooks and a plastic envelope of origami paper. I ruffle through the sheets and pull out a yellow square.

"I can do these in under a minute now."

"Yeah? Okay, show me. I'll time you."

Micky pulls out her iPhone. She plays with the screen and smiles. "Go!"

Quickly and gently, I fold the creases on the sheet. One square becomes two triangles. Two triangles become four. Unfold. Follow the crease on both sides to make a square. Fold the bottom halves to make a diamond. Unfold.

"Not a lot of people coming in today, eh Mick?"

"No. I guess 'cause reading week's coming up. People don't really have a lot of exams. I'll probably close up pretty soon."

I flatten the diamond, open the top flap, and fold on the creases. Take the bottom half and fold into the tail and head. Unhinge the wings, unwind the tail, unstraighten the beak.

"What's that?"

"Fifty-five seconds. Not bad, Jay."

"At this rate, I can get them done by three. I'll probably have to wait 'til tomorrow to send them out anyway."

"Where is she again? Newfoundland?"

"Nova Scotia. SFX."

"You think it can get there by Valentine's Day?"

"Well, I can do rush delivery or one-day delivery. I can get a giant box from No Frills and dress it up before tomorrow. Put a big bow on it or something."

A girl knocks. "Are you guys still open? Do you have a past exam for Psych 220?"

"Sure. Let me get that for you," Micky says. "Just have a seat next to the paper guy over there."

She hovers over the couch and stares at the dozens of cranes on the table. "Project?"

"Sort of. More like a Valentine's Day project."

Micky returns with the exam and hands it to the student. "More like a romantic comedy kind of project," she says.

Every other day, at 11:11 p.m., for the past month and a half, I wait for a phone call from Leona. She always calls at 11:11. Whenever the phone rings, I smile. Whenever she says "Hi," I know she's smiling, too. I liken our conversations to Meg Ryan and Tom Hanks. We share jokes from our favourite romantic comedies. We listen to each other's heartbreaks, past breakups, could've beens, should've beens, would've beens.

We met during a camping trip. We sang by the campfire. I met her cute, plush teddy bear, Leo. On our first night out in the city, we watched *P.S. I Love You.* She cried, I held her. Then she went back to school. Now she lives a long, costly plane ride away. The fifteen cent per minute long-distance calls gets us through.

"Why 11:11?" I ask.

"Well, at 11:11, you always make a wish."

"What would you wish for?"

"I don't know. I can't just have one. I have too many wishes."

"I guess we all do."

I listen to her smooth, sultry, cheerful voice as she lists her wishes. She wants peace, justice, happiness, and passing grades on her upcoming midterms. She laughs awkwardly and politely when she realizes she has talked for fourteen minutes without me saying a word. I laugh with her.

"There's also this one legend that if you make one thousand cranes, you can make any wish you want, and a crane will grant it to you. So, whenever I get down, I start making paper cranes. Maybe I can make a wish."

"You finished a thousand?" I ask.

"No. I've been doing it for years, but I only got up to about eight hundred. I guess it would take anybody a while to get to one thousand. What about you? What would you wish for?"

"I don't know. I might have too many as well. I'll let you know when I figure it out. You already make my wish come true when you call."

"You're so cheesy."

"I know."

She hangs up. I climb into my bed and clutch my pillow. Our conversations make sleeping easy.

Three days after Valentine's Day, I return home after reading week and listen to my voicemail. I hear Leona's voice. She's smiling. I drop my luggage, hurry to my room, and search for my calling card. I dial and wait.

"Hello?"

"Hey, Leona."

"Hi! Where've you been? I went to the post office to pick up this ridiculously large package from the most amazing person ever. Thank you."

"Glad you liked it. Did you enjoy your Valentine's Day?"

"You made it great. What did you wish for?"

"Well, you just had too many wishes, so I wished for all of your wishes to come true."

She laughs.

We wait in calm, comfortable, confident silence.

"You're so cheesy."

"I know."

"You made 1,017 cranes."

"Oh, I actually went over?"

"Yeah. Those seventeen are my favourites."

Chapter 5: People

*Use details of action, speech and setting
to present a person you know.*

The Unexpected Birthday Present

Justin Lau

I count out one thousand five hundred dollars and slide the bills into a Toronto-Dominion bank envelope while I watch reruns of *Friends*.

I wait for Dan's call.

My house phone rings.

"Hello?"

"I'm near your house."

"Alright, I'll be there in a second." I hang up the phone, grab the envelope and head out the door. The sun beams on a hot June afternoon. I stroll along Crawford Street, towards Queen. Ahead, pedestrians, cyclists and cars flood the street. I approach Dan near the intersection and hand him the bank envelope. He tucks it under his jersey, stands with his back towards Queen, and counts the money.

I lend Dan money to help him grow his drug business.

Dan stands six feet tall with a skinny frame. He wears light grey jeans, a white 76ers Allen Iverson jersey, a white Yankees cap and white Air Force 1 running shoes. A silver Ruff Ryders chain dangles around his neck and a silver watch rests on his right wrist.

Dan reeks of marijuana and cigarette smoke.

"Respect," Dan says. "What have you been up to?"

"Not much…just school. How about you?"

"Same old, same old. Hustle hard and stack paper."

We stand beside the Candy Factory Lofts in the shade of two large trees. A half-foot-high concrete border surrounds a garden that blooms with a wide range of flowers. We use the concrete garden wall as a seat.

"Your fifteenth birthday just passed, didn't it?" Dan asks.

"Yeah," I say. "Last week."

"Nice. Let's celebrate. Let's go to a whorehouse."

"Sure." I laugh. "Why not?"

"I wasn't joking."

I stare into Dan's bloodshot eyes and he stares back. I look away. My eyes fixate on the date—02/14/04—engraved on his watch. On that day, Dan and Vanessa, his girlfriend of over a year, started seeing each other.

Vanessa is smart, funny, hardworking, and beautiful. Her family lives in Regent Park, a ghetto in Toronto's east end. She works two part-time jobs to help out her single mom and younger sister. She makes the honour roll every semester. Vanessa has long black hair, a round face and a big, bright, beautiful smile. Most of Dan's friends call her "the Asian Girl with Huge Knockers."

"Wait…you wanna go to a whorehouse? What about Vanessa? Why would you cheat on her?"

"It's not cheating if she doesn't find out."

"What if she finds out?"

"She won't."

"But what if?"

"Then she does. It's just sex. It's not cheating," Dan says. "Cheating is when you're *with* another girl. It's different from fucking another girl. Besides, fucking other girls makes me better at sex, so in the end, Vanessa will be happy, too. Think of it like a video game. You're level one. Whores are level ninety-nine. They help you level up."

I laugh and cover my face with my hand.

"Did you really just compare sex to a video game? Alright, alright, alright. So I'm level one. I'm not in a rush to reach level ninety-nine. I'm fifteen years old. I don't plan on trading my virginity for a couple of STDs. That doesn't sound like a good deal."

"You don't fuck them raw dog style. You don't kiss them. You don't even have to talk to them. You just put on a condom and bang them. That's it." Dan chuckles. "Look, when you get a girlfriend, you're gonna wanna please her, right? I'm helping you get a head start."

"Of course. But with your logic, I could sleep with anyone who's higher than level one to reach a higher level, right? Tell your mom to holla at cha boy then," I say.

"You're a sick fuck. My mom is old."

Dan makes a fist and punches my shoulder. My shoulder stings from his all-bone knuckles and the large diamond ring on his middle finger. I laugh, and grimace.

"Look, it was just an example," I say. "I don't want to sleep with a prostitute. I can't. It's wrong."

"It's not wrong. You're helping them. It's their job."

"I don't know how to explain it. I just can't do it."

"Stop being a little bitch."

"Fuck you." I laugh. "I'm not going."

"Fine. I'll just go with someone else."

"What the fuck? You're still going? I thought you were going for my birthday. How the fuck is this a birthday present if you're going to go anyway?"

"I was going to pay for you."

"With the money I just lent you? That's like paying for my own prostitute that I never wanted in the first place."

I sigh. Thank God there's no one around to eavesdrop.

"I'm paying you back," Dan says. "I'd also let you have first pick."

"Oh, wow. I'm honoured. Are the girls even good looking? How much is it?"

"Some of them are. It's around eighty dollars."

Dan reaches into his right pocket. He grabs his Belmonts and Zippo lighter and removes a cigarette from the pack. He places the cigarette between his lips and lights it. Dan flashes the "THUG LIFE" engraving on the body of the Zippo at me. He inhales and shoots out grey smoke.

"Hold on," I say. "So you're telling me that you're going to pay for me, with the money I just lent you, and you're going to give me the first pick of the girls, who may or may not be good looking? Fuck that. It would be at least more convincing if they were good looking. It's not worth paying for sex unless the girl looks like Jessica Alba, and even then, it's still wrong."

Dan laughs. "Whatever. I'm still going. It's not worth paying eighty dollars for you to last two minutes in her anyway."

"First of all, it's not two minutes. It's more like two minutes and ten and a half seconds. Don't cut me short on those ten and a half seconds. That shit can make a difference. Second of all, fuck you."

Dan grins. "Alright man, I'm out. I'll call you this weekend."

"Alright. Have fun."

We shake hands, lean in, and pat each other once on the back. Dan struts to the cluttered corner of Queen and Crawford and flags down a taxi. An orange and green Beck pulls over. Dan hops in and the cab drives off.

Bill

Selina Africaine

A small crowd gathers around Mr. Ram, the headmaster, and Bill, my brother, in the sixth standard classroom. Bill, my sister Janet and I attend St. Pius Roman Catholic School in Georgetown, Guyana.

Mr. Ram and I hate each other. I don't know when the animosity between Mr. Ram and I began. I just know that he hates me and wants me out of his school, and I hate him and I wish he would kick me out.

At home, Bill and I don't get along. He wants to be big and he hates that I'm a year older than him. I just turned ten and Bill nine. But outside the confines of our home, I protect Bill. I fight for him, and he fights for me. We have our own friends and hardly play together, but we support each other.

I quickly enter the open doorway. I see fear on Bill's face. His bloodshot eyes fill with unshed tears. Rage darkens Mr. Ram's face. His nostrils flare and oily sweat drips down his forehead from his greasy straight hair. His new cane will soon be in his hand and landing on Bill's backside.

I'm convinced Mr. Ram, a short, dark-skinned East Indian, hates all the black students at St. Pius. Every black child who ever got into trouble knows how cruel the headmaster can be. Once in a while, a furious black parent comes to the school aiming to do to Mr. Ram what he did to their child. Each time, we all gather around expecting to see Mr. Ram get his due, but he can be as slippery as an eel. He greets the parent with such warmth and shows such care for the welfare of their kid. He talks about how he wants what's best for their child and that's why he must be strict. The parent ends up leaving the meeting angry with their kid and apologizing to Mr. Ram.

With fear and excitement on their faces, students gather around Bill and Mr. Ram. I stand at the fringe of the crowd, afraid to get closer in case Mr. Ram sees me. I have never seen Bill look so scared. I know he doesn't want to cry in front of all the students. He looks trapped, the headmaster determined.

"Bend over!" Mr. Ram speaks softly and yet somehow his voice booms in the hushed silence.

"Please, sir." My mouth opens on its own accord, the words just popping out. "Please don't beat Bill. Last night he had a fever."

Mr. Ram turns towards me. His face gets darker. Two veins pulse on his oily forehead. His lizard-like yellow eyes fix on me.

"What did you say?"

"Bill, sir." My lisp worsens and my tongue feels heavy. "He had a fever last night."

"Come here!"

I look at Bill as I move forward. He wipes away the tears that have spilled down his cheeks.

"Please, sir. I'll take Bill's licks for him." I force the words out of my dry mouth. "He won't do it again."

Mr. Ram looks at me. He seems amused and even smiles. "Okay, Mary. Bend over."

I bend over the desk and hold my skirt close to me.

"One."

Oh, God! The lash hurts more than any he has given me before, as if the cane cuts through the flesh to my bone.

"Two."

Sweet Jesus, I can't take it. I feel hot pee run down my legs.

"Three."

Screams pour forth from my mouth. When I think I can bear it no longer and will faint, the lashes stop.

"Get out!" Mr. Ram orders. "Get out!"

I straighten up from the desk. My body trembles all over.

"Bend over!"

A gasp escapes from everyone's mouth. I stop and turn around. Bill bends over the desk. Mr. Ram's hand reaches high in the air. The cane gleams.

I feel hatred, blind hatred. I taste bile rising to my throat. I feel helpless, devastated, defeated, overwhelmed, worthless. I turn and walk out of the room and towards the front doors of St. Pius. As I step down the stairs, I see the green sugarcane fields in the distance. I wish I could lose myself there, where no one will ever find me.

~~~

Years later, I'm a new immigrant in Canada. I apply for a course in nursing. I need a recommendation from my old school. I write Mr. Ram. I hope he has forgotten me and will write a recommendation for a faceless past student.

Mr. Ram's reply comes promptly. I feel excited as I tear open the envelope. I picture myself in a nurse's uniform. I imagine my mother's face when I write and tell her I have been accepted to nursing school.

> *To whom it may concern,*
> *I cannot in good conscience recommend Mary to*
> *a fine profession like nursing. She is the most dif-*
> *ficult student I have ever encountered in my years of*
> *teaching. She was an undisciplined troublemaker, a*
> *cantankerous and vicious child, a child, who....*

The letter drops out of my trembling hands. Sobs shake my body. I feel as hopeless, useless and worthless as I did when Mr. Ram had beaten me as a child. I sit on the floor and cry. I cry until I can cry no more.

Then I tear up the letter and the application form for nursing college.

Buried the Jewish Way

Natasha Segal

We don't have ten men for the *minyan*. So we opt out of a synagogue service. Rabbi Zaltzman says he will try and get some people he knows to come and help carry the casket. A Jew needs ten men to carry his casket. Dyedushka didn't have ten male friends left.

We prop Babushka on a bench inside the cemetery. She can't make the long walk to the grave. As the small procession of old ladies from the building gathers around the open hole that awaits Dyedushka's body, Babushka sits and faces the sun alone.

The hearse arrives. The men who carry Dyedushka's casket barely know him; old men from his building, tricked into the job by friendly old ladies from down the hall. Their legs wobble, bow shaped, their shoulders sag beneath the casket's solid weight. Sweat pours off their wrinkled foreheads and stains the collars of their wrinkled shirts. They grit their dentures, smile strong smiles for the half-blind old ladies, and grip the edges of the plain pine box.

"Can I help?" I ask Rabbi Zaltzman.

"No, no." He waves me away.

I follow the old men's grunts down the hill to the hole. Three rabbis arrive. I only know Rabbi Zaltzman. I stand in silence at the front of the small crowd. Mama stands beside me. Behind us, the ladies of 3638 Bathurst Street fiddle with flowers and hairpins and hats. The rabbis wince at the flowers. Jews don't bring flowers to funerals.

Rabbi Zaltzman leans on a gravestone. His black eyes scan the scant congregation. His beard has grown grey since we first met. The rabbi wears a black hat, long black coat, shiny black shoes, black pants and black shirt. All black, all the time. A *Chasid*—a strict Orthodox Jew.

"I have known Mikhail, Misha, since I was …." Rabbi Zaltzman pats a spot beside his hip. "He always reminded me that we came from the same little village in Russia. Always when I saw him I would say, 'Misha, how are you today?' and he always smiled, always smiled and said, 'Very well. I am very well!' And that is how I remember Mikhail. He was always joyful and happy to see you."

A lump forms in my throat. My vision blurs.

Rabbi Zaltzman calls Mama. She stumbles over a patch of green grass and reaches the front.

"What can I say, he was a good father—the best, the best father… I am sorry…I cannot say anymore."

Rabbi Zaltzman extends his open hand to me. I look into his eyes and shake my head.

"Say something for your grandfather," he says.

Again, I shake my head. Slow—the grass moves so slow.

"Are you sure?" the rabbi says.

I nod.

I called Rabbi Zaltzman yesterday morning.

"I need to speak to Rabbi Zaltzman right now," I told his secretary.

"He is a busy man. Can I take a message?"

"I need him now," I said.

"May I ask what this is about?"

"My grandfather just died."

"Oh…oh my, of course. I will go and tell him." She left me in the dead call-waiting air.

"Natasha," Rabbi Zaltzman's familiar voice, calm and slow, came over the telephone line.

"*Dyedushka umer*," I stammered. "Dyedushka died." The Russian word for "grandfather" rolled from my throat, broken between sobs, jolted on half-forgotten words. "He was a father to me, he raised me—Rabbi, I don't know what to do."

"You are in charge of the arrangements?" Rabbi Zaltzman asks.

"I guess."

"Will your mother be helping?"

"I don't know."

"Do you want me to call her?"

"I want to bury him the Jewish way."

"Of course," Rabbi Zaltzman replied. "We will handle everything."

Silence.

"What hospital is he in?"

"Sunnybrook."

"I will send someone there right now."

I leaned over my kitchen counter and wretched. My breath stopped. My eyes burned.

"Thank you," I croaked.

"Yes," Rabbi Zaltzman said. "Jews must be buried as soon as possible. We will bury him tomorrow. I will call your mother."

Today, frail old men shovel brown dirt over a casket that sits snug down inside the hole. The women watch. The rabbis pray. The crowd throws handfuls of grey rocks and soil into the wound. I grab a shovel. I shovel great shovelfuls of dirt into the grave.

"Who are you?" hollers some old man behind me. "Did you know him?"

"I'm his granddaughter," I say over my shoulder.

"Women aren't allowed to shovel dirt into the grave—we're Jews here."

I turn and hand him the shovel. He touches my shovel and then lets it fall to the ground.

"You useless fucking motherfucker!" I scream. The crowd freezes. "You want me to throw you into the fucking grave, too, you piece of shit, you bastard? You wanna see who's the real man around here, you want me to fucking show you?"

I strip off my shawl.

"I'll kill you, you useless fucking pig. Who the fuck invited you here! Who *am* I? Who the fuck *am* I? You want me to show you who the fuck I am?" I shake. My face burns. "Come closer, bitch! Come closer so we can show everyone who the fuck the real man is—you fuck, you useless stupid old fuck!"

"Natashinka." Mama's fingers flutter over my shoulder. "Your babushka is all alone on the bench. You should go and keep her company."

"Fuck you, you bitch!" I spit. "You go and keep her company."

The old man looks to Rabbi Zaltzman. "I'm just an old man at a funeral," he chokes.

"Soon it'll be your fucking funeral!" I say. "Learn to shut the fuck up before I shut you the fuck up."

"I'm just a man at a funeral."

"You're just a fucking piece of shit, is what you are."

Yesterday afternoon I arrived at the intensive care ward at the exact same time as Mama and Babushka. The nurse looked at me quizzically as I barged through the hospital doors.

"She is my daughter, Mikhail's granddaughter," Mama said. "She is with us."

We marched to bed number thirteen. We formed a half-moon around Dyedushka's feet. Without his teeth, he didn't look like Dyedushka. A nurse slipped through two closed hospital curtains. She talked—really fast—into Mama's ear.

"Explain to her," Mama pointed at me. "We do not understand your English."

I stood up, straightened myself, and faced the nurse, forcing myself to make eye contact. The nurse stumbled backwards through the curtains and mumbled something. I pulled a footstool beside Babushka's chair and sat by her swollen feet.

A rabbi came by.

"Ms. Sigalov? I am here from the funeral home. Rabbi Zaltzman sent me. I will make sure that everything goes by the Jewish rules with the body."

The body.

"They have already done more than we allow, according to the Jewish laws," he said and tilted his head. We nodded.

"I will perform some initial prayers now." The rabbi pulled out a small black siddur from a blue velvet pouch. He opened the book, then sauntered to the corner of our makeshift room and stood by Dyedushka's head, the sun to his back. He prayed in Hebrew, a fast, melodious chant. He chanted us into a new world, a world without Dyedushka. He said "amen" when he was done, but it wasn't in unison with ours.

Then the rabbi wheeled Dyedushka's bed toward the curtain.

"I will take him and wash him and pray over him and bring him to the funeral site tomorrow," he said. Babushka nodded.

The rabbi told us it was time to go. We rose, gathered our things, and left.

Diamond Heights

Rachel James

"'ve come to take you. I've come to take you."

I sing the words like a ghost as I take my 101-year-old grand-mother's hands and pull her arms gently towards me.

"I should stand up, but…"

I bend down and position her feet. We prepare for the ascent out of the chair. Grandma Trilby looks towards the window, at her make-believe audience.

"Stand up, lady!" Her voice booms baritone.

"Stand up!" I say in our make-believe opera.

"You don't want to pee in your pants!" Grandma finishes the phrase, motionless in her chair. "Oh, everything is…"

"Work?" I offer.

"Everything is *difficult*. Standing up. Sitting down. Going to bed. Now getting up." She takes a breath, then exhales. "I can't get up."

I lean in and wrap my arms around her in a bear hug. I lift her, careful not to pull or push on anything. I become an extension of her body.

"I know how. Just take my word for it," I say.

"I know you know how," she says, sounding annoyed. Grandma resists at first, then rises.

"Okay, run for it." Grandma hobbles in the direction my hands lead her. At first her wide gait looks stiff. Her body rocks side to side as if she were a cardboard cutout of herself.

"Step," I announce and she lifts a foot over the metal lip separating the living room carpet from the kitchen tile.

Grandma was born Esther Levitsky. Soon after birth, she was diagnosed with severe rickets. Her mother, Bubbe Razel, placed Esther waist-high in cow manure and left her there for three days. She was cured. Six years later, Esther and her four siblings, her mother and father and two uncles, boarded a ship in Russia and sailed to New York. They all lived in a one-bedroom tenement—a common sight on Hopkinson Avenue in 1912.

"Step," I say again to Grandma, at the lip of the bathroom tile.

After eleven years in Brooklyn as Esther, Grandma decided to choose her own name, Trilby, from *Svengali*. Grandma had played the part in a grade-school play. Trilby—the diva entranced by the evil hypnotist—could find a job. Trilby wasn't a Jewish name.

"Good luck," I say and place Grandma's hand on the bathroom sink.

Trilby studied modern dance under dance pioneers Martha Graham and Doris Humphrey.

Grandma steadies herself. I step back. I feel like a creepy voyeur. I make sure she pulls her pants all the way down, and then I walk out. I track her progress in the bathroom from the kitchen. I stare out the window above the sink. The sun has set and the lights that line the city below warp through the old windowpanes. I love San Francisco for the hills, for the fog that rolls in unannounced, for the constant hide-and-seek of the coast below.

Grandpa Elfryn built Grandma's rickety wooden house at the top of a hill in Diamond Heights. He died fifty-one years ago. Grandma Trilby has lived in the house without Grandpa Elfryn for more years than she had lived with him. The one-bedroom house stands out on the block. Once surrounded by eucalyptus trees and farmland, it now sits awkwardly between three-storey mansions and perfectly manicured lawns.

I walk back into the bathroom. Grandma rests with her eyes closed and rubs a spot on her scalp with her right hand. I grab a tin of shea butter from the shelf. I nail a chunk out and smear it on my palm. I warm it up in quick circular motions. It turns from paste to oil. I dab it on the scabs lining the side of her scalp.

"You know, I'll tell you, Rachel, there's a lot that happens in life that you can't put your finger on it now." Grandma knocks the dentures out of her mouth with her tongue and hands them to me. I rinse them under the running tap. "But just get much older, you can be younger than I am, and they suddenly appear. Things like, my brother used to play the violin—this was the First World War—and he would play for the soldiers who were maimed."

I wrap toilet paper around the four fingers on my left hand.

"My brother took me for years. I must have blocked it out of my mind and now I know why."

I hand Grandma the wad of toilet paper and begin rolling a new one.

"Do you know all they had was their torsos? And they put them in bird cages and they were hanging all around the walls of the warehouse on meat hooks."

"In cages?" I respond. I wrap my arms around her and lift her from the toilet seat. She keeps her legs spread apart and begins to wipe.

"That was the First World War! All they had was here-to-here; no arms, no legs. And it affected me so…that I wiped it out of my memory."

I slip the second wad of toilet paper off my fingers. I peer into the toilet bowl—dark, hard pebbles. Not bad, I think. At least there's something. I wipe Grandma's butt and drop the wad into the toilet, She flushes.

"And it came back now, it all comes back now, everything that's happened."

"Why do you think it comes back?" I ask.

"Because you try so hard to forget it."

I hand Grandma her toothbrush. She still has four teeth, two on top and two on the bottom.

"I wish I could have met some of your friends," I say through a mouth full of white suds. I decided to brush my teeth, too. My words come out garbled.

Grandma spits into the sink.

"Well, when I was young, you know, still in public school, I had Bella Puro and Gertrude Ruben. They were my best friends, the two of them. Gertrude Ruben and Bella Puro. And Florence Lipschitz! The three. This was in Brooklyn."

Grandma dries each finger methodically.

"The Lipschitz' were the aristocrats. And she befriended *me*? I stuck my chest out!"

Grandma shuts her eyes and shuffles slowly toward her bedroom, gliding her hands along the wall. She reaches out for the top of the radiator to navigate through the doorframe. Grandma keeps her eyes closed.

I walk into the bedroom before her and stand beside the remote-controlled single bed. I pull the top sheet down and the blankets fold with it. I rearrange the three pillows. Grandma sits on the edge of the bed. I bend to help her raise her left calf. We swing together, aiming for the centre of the bed. I hand Grandma her *Codewords* book and a pen.

Chocolate hides above the refrigerator. If she eats too much, Grandma's scalp itches unbearably. She knows this, but still it's a fight. I unwrap a bar as quietly as I can and pop three squares into my mouth. I find the phone under a dishtowel and dial home.

"Hello?" Dad picks up.

"Hey, it's me. Is it too late?" Toronto is three hours ahead.

"No, we're just lying here. How's it going out there?"

"Good, but Grandma only had a tiny shit today. Rabbit poo."

"Put the cilium in her morning shake."

I open the pantry door. "What does it look like?"

Dad and I talk for a while, but I can tell he was sleeping when I called. He agrees to pick me up at the airport on Sunday. I imagine being back in my apartment: laundry, midterms, work at the bar, a lover I barely like. My bike is broken and the fridge will be empty.

I find Grandma asleep, chin to chest. I lean in and press my cheek softly against hers. She stiffens for a moment, then sighs, knowing it is me without opening her eyes. Her flesh is more forgiving than mine.

"Come in," she growls. "There's room."

"Okay."

She hacks into a tissue she pulls from her sleeve. I take the tissue and toss it into the wastebasket beside her bed.

"Let's watch something," she says.

Grandma can barely make out the images on the TV screen. I take the wireless earphones off the bedside table and click the power switch on. I hand them to Grandma. She bends them open and inches them into her ears like a stethoscope.

"Is it a talkie?" she asks.

"Silent. But it's Greta Garbo—and she's young!"

"Oh, my."

Grandma listens to the lonely call of a single violin crescendo. Garbo twirls frantically around a mob of masked characters. A clarinet sounds through the chaos, depicting the carnivalesque masquerade.

"She sees a man," I yell, pulling out her left earphone. "They take their masks off! She's enchanted with him!"

"Oh, right." Grandma laughs. "I think I know this one."

~~~

"Hello?" I know Grandma answers her phone in the living room. She never picks up when she's in her bedroom.

"Grandma, it's Rachel." I strain to be both loud and relaxed. "How are you?"

"Oh, Rachel. I'm the last rose of summer."

"I've been writing down the stories you told me when I visited last," I say.

She laughs. "Well, everything changes, my dear, in one's mind."

"How do you mean?"

"Each day is not the same when you get to my age. What happened then and what you think now, each day it's different."

Mortal Fear

John Currie

I play in a band called Mortal Fear. We create our own brand of heavy rock and breed it with a touch of class. I like the name Mortal Fear, not only because it suits the genre, but because it means fear of death or fear of living life to its fullest, or some combination of the two. I ponder the possibilities of a band named Mortal Fear.

Two brothers, Pete and Steve, the core of Fear, play guitar and bass. We all have long hair and write tunes with solid hooks. We practise three days a week at the Haines Road rehearsal room. We party and jam. People talk about the show at the Plantation Bowlerama and Ballroom for months. They tell us how we smoked Savage Steel—who has three albums to our none—off the stage.

Ten years later, Pete, Steve and I still have long hair, except my baldness shows. I am now twenty-seven, Pete twenty-six and Steve thirty-one. We've all been in different bands over the years since Mortal Fear disbanded. Steve joined Savage Steel and recorded a CD, so his ego is huge. I'm glad he's not my brother.

To play together again ten years later feels right. We still love to play loud rock. After a few good jams in my basement, we create a smokin' new original.

We rent rehearsal space, a twenty-by-thirty-foot graffiti-covered room in Etobicoke on Royal York Road, for three hundred bucks a month. Black magic marker drawings cover the walls: a torna-do spins a house, cow and car across the room; a short black man smokes a big joint; a huge skinhead peers out from behind dark glasses. Some poet has scrawled:

Roses are red, violets are blue.
I'm a schizophrenic and so am I.

Another has written, "Lord Hell Puss."

Pete, Steve and I move in and set up a dingy yellow couch, a few plastic chairs, garbage cans, ashtrays and a tape deck. We lay some PA cabinets on their sides to make a table.

I feel excited to set up my drums again. A drum riser gives my drums good sound, the height I need to be at eye level with the rest of the band and that overall pro feel to things. I put new drum skins on, airbrushed with Mortal Fear in blue and silver on a black background. The reunion begins. To celebrate, I buy a metronome.

The band practises three nights a week, originals only, no covers. We create songs and plan to record them. In three months we have five solid new originals. We also resurrect two classics: "Homicide" and "The Frantic Waltz."

On Fridays, just like the old days, friends come down to the room to watch us. They drink and give us feedback about our music and cheer at the end of each song when they're drunk. Pat, the land-lord, who also plays in a band, comes by and tells us we're good. Our crowd grows.

I drive down to the room alone three days a week, practise my drums, scribble lyrics on notepads and think about designing T-shirts, business cards and even a website. I hope to use my marketing background and have some fun, too.

On a March weeknight evening, I go to practise my drums. I pull up and see Steve's grey minivan parked outside. I walk down the stairs past the video games to our room, the third black door on the left. The door is locked. I hear feet scuffle. As I put my key in, Steve opens the door. His face looks white and his eyes bulge.

"Oh, it's John," Steve says. Pete sits at the stereo and puts something away.

"What's going on?" I ask.

"Nothing."

"Why are you guys here?"

"Oh, we just wanted to smoke a joint. Does it smell in here?"

"No."

"Are you sure?"

"Yes. What kind of joint?"

"Hash. So, you can't smell anything?"

"Yeah, that's right. I know what hash smells like and I don't smell a thing."

"Well, we gotta get going. See ya later, John."

The brothers gather their jackets and leave. I bash my drums for the next hour.

The next practice night I'm the first to get to the room. Just as I slip into my drumming shoes, Steve bursts in. "Listen John, I'm just going to smoke a joint before we play, okay? I don't want any of your fuckin' lectures or anything. I've had a shitty day at work and I just need to relax, okay?"

Steve and Pete work at Wolfedale Auto Parts. Steve drives parts around, Pete works the front counter. They've been there for five years. I know they make ten bucks an hour and drink it all during their lunch hours and still live at home and don't pay any rent. I know how they've partied over the years. Steve and Pete know I'm back in school.

"Okay," I say.

Pete comes in and says to his brother, "Ah, can't you fuckin' wait 'til later, man?"

"No!" Steve half whines, half screams. "Sit down, John," he says. "You're making me nervous."

I sit and watch in silence as Steve takes out some foil and reveals something that looks like baby teeth.

"What the fuck is that?" I shout. "It's fuckin' crack, isn't it? What the fuck are you doing?"

"I knew we shouldn't have done it in front of John, man!" says Pete.

"Calm down, calm down," Steve says to me. "It's powder."

"Powder?"

"Relax, man. It's coke powder. I've been doing it for years in lines. It irritates my nose, so I smoke it now."

"Wha—"

"LOOK, JUST SHUT UP OKAY. I'm just going to relax and then we'll play, okay? Why don't you sit down and tell me about what you're studying."

I pause. Steve's never given a shit about what I do at university. But I'm ablaze with the stuff I'm learning in my religion classes. Professor McMullin's way of looking at the politics and psychology of religion has made me think about the world differently.

I like being listened to. I talk for the next two hours.

Throughout, the brothers suck bitter-smelling smoke from a Coke can. They inhale from the pull-tab opening. Near the base of the can they've made a dent and six or seven pinholes. A cigarette always burns nearby. Steve and Pete put cigarette ashes in the dent and then place tiny pieces of crack on the ashes. They light it and inhale.

Steve enters big brother mode and orders Pete to prepare a haul for him. While Pete complies, Steve tells him to be quiet, the cops might be around.

For two hours the Coke can touches the dry lips of the brothers. The whiff of drugs haunts the dark hole of a room. The music of the past fades from the band's mind. The air is laden with fear. I talk aloud of the lyrical rapture of the words "Mortal Fear" and on how religion has caused many wars. Steve asks me why I study it and I tell him that it's like history, and between hauls he wants to know where studying history is going to get me.

I speak on and on. I feel trapped in a soliloquy. I stop.

Steve's and Pete's eyes have become glossy, their pupils huge. The two have smoked a "fifty piece" in two hours.

"What was that?" Pete says at nothing.

I follow the brothers' spiralling gazes to the filth on the beer-stained carpet. I smell the bitter, acrid smoke as the cloud sinks into the room.

As he waits for his haul Steve mumbles, "Don't worry, man, I'm listening. Keep talking."

Silence.

Steve stands and wavers. "Can I do this next haul from behind your drums, man?"

I rise, walk to my drums, seize my jean jacket, put it on, and march out. I storm down the concrete hallway, past the video games, up the wooden stairs, through the metal door, out into the parking lot. I breathe the crisp night air and find my car with the light of the streetlamps.

~~~

A week later I return to the rehearsal room and find it empty, except for my drums, the graffiti and a dead mouse in the middle of the room. I put the mouse in the garbage.

I play my drums. I play well. I plan to find another band, write lyrics, create originals, market the band, and have fun. There are other good names out there.

Counting Time

Sami Karaman

I'm supposed to meet with my friends soon. Marco said he'd pick me up at nine. We're going to chill at Matt's house in the Batcave. I wait outside for Marco. It's nine. Whenever Marco's late, I walk up the street and cut him off. I get to the stop sign at the end of Strata Court and wait with my hands on my hips. I see headlights in the darkness. Marco pulls up near me in a blue Hyundai. I open the door.

"What's up, buddy?" Marco says. He wears slim cut jeans and a Guess shirt. His black hair is gelled, pointing upwards at the front. The radio blares "Hell Ya, Fucking Right" by Drake.

"You're late." I turn down the radio.

"Whatever," he says. "So, what the fuck we doin' tonight?"

"No clue," I say. "I just wanna chill."

"What's in the bag?"

"Snacks."

"You're a ridiculous human being."

Marco makes a three-point turn and drives through my neighbourhood. As usual, we hit a red light at Winston Churchill Boulevard.

"Just run it."

He runs through the red light as he always does. "Fuckin' light takes forever, dawg."

"Yeah," I say. "So, you seen Christina since you got back from vacay?"

Marco smirks, rubs his chin. He doesn't like talking about his personal life. I don't understand why. I tell my friends everything.

"What's the big deal," I press on. "You're a guy, she's a girl. Your hormones make you want to—"

"Yeah, yeah, I've seen her," he says. "So what?"

Marco makes a right onto Derry Road. I sit further up in my seat. "Well, what did you guys do?"

"We made out and shit," he says.

"And shit as in…?"

"Nothing, nothing," he says. "We didn't do anything."

"Where were you?"

"My basement."

"At night?"

"Yeah, yeah. My parents were asleep."

"You guys were alone in your basement at night, making out, and you couldn't close? What the fuck, man?"

"I know, dude." Marco makes a right onto Tenth Line. "I don't know. Like, we kissed, and then all of a sudden she's saying she wants a relationship and stuff, and I just freaked out."

"What did you say?"

"I just kept saying, 'I don't know, I don't know,' to everything. She went crazy, like, she starts crying and cuddling me and shit, and says she sees a psychiatrist because she was taken advantage of in her other relationship or some bullshit. Fuck me, man. Fuck me."

"True," I say.

Marco makes a left into Matt's complex.

"Well, maybe you should date her."

"Fuck that," he says. He parks in the visitors' parking space.

"Why not?" I ask, opening my door. "Aren't we at that age where, like, we gotta find someone?"

"I guess so."

We walk up the street. Marco points at my grey hoodie and grey sweatpants. "Man, you're wearing a fuckin' onesie right now."

"Yeah, whatever, like I give a shit. I'm wearing grey socks too. Wait till we get inside."

"You're a ridiculous human being."

Matt is a very precise person. He never wants us to have any kind of conversation with his parents in case it becomes awkward. So he opens his garage door and waits to escort us into the Batcave. Marco and I walk up his driveway and into the garage. Matt stands on a set of stairs that leads into his basement. He wears a Yankees cap and pyjamas. His skin is tanned, his eyes big and blue. He sees us and looks down at his BlackBerry, probably to text his girlfriend, Monica.

"'Sup, buddy?" Marco says.

"What's in the bag?" Matt asks me.

"My food." A twelve-pack sits on the ground next to the stairs. "I'm takin' a Coke," I say and reach into the box and grab a can. The three of us walk inside to the basement. We step down another staircase into a small, cold, dark room and reach the Batcave. I sit at my spot in the armchair.

"It's always fuckin' me," Marco says. He walks to the light fixture. A string should be attached, but I broke it about a year ago. Now, to turn it on and off, we just spin the light bulb in and out of the socket. He turns it and light bursts through the room.

Matt and Marco sit across from me on a couch. A rectangular table sits between us. On the wall to our left is a toy basketball net we toss a small ball into from time to time. A washing machine and a dryer sit next to a big, ugly sink in the far corner of the room.

I pick up Matt's acoustic guitar and strum. "Your guitar actually sounds alright today. It's usually shit."

"I tuned it." He picks up a deck of cards from the table and starts shuffling.

"You're a dick," Marco says to me and smiles.

"I'm just saying. There's some good guitars, then there's some not-so-good guitars. And this one's—"

"Not-so-good," Matt and Marco say together.

"I know, dude," Matt says. "I get it. I got it for Christmas. It's my first one."

"I know, I know," I say innocently. "Hey, it's decent. It's not terrible. I mean, my guitar's pretty shit, too. It's a Samick. Like, what the fuck kind of name for a company is that?"

"Why don't you buy a new one?" Marco asks.

"I don't got money for that, man," I say. "Maybe when I'm done school. One more year, you know, till I'm working full time in some shit office and making coffee for the boss, or the hot girl, or whoever the fuck gets to make me do that shit."

"Oh yeah," Matt says. "You graduate this year."

"Yeah. You guys are dumb. I don't know why you'd slow the process down. I just want to get on with life, you know?"

"What are we going to do when he's gone?" Matt taps Marco on the arm.

"Do you know any new tricks?" Marco asks, pointing to the deck in Matt's hand. Matt thinks he's a magician. He posts magic tricks on YouTube.

"Yeah, I made a good one." He puffs his chest and rolls up his sleeves. "Want me to do it now?"

"Whatever," I say. I slouch in my armchair and eat my beef patty sandwich.

"Dude," Matt says. "Are you seriously wearing all grey right now?"

I raise my feet and show them my grey socks. Through a mouthful I say, "Who gives a fuck. Honestly, am I at a goddamn wedding right now?"

"It's okay, it's okay," Marco says. He raises a hand at me. "He's a ridiculous human being. Start the trick."

"Okay," Matt says. "So, this is only going to happen once. Okay?" He looks at Marco. Marco nods.

Letting Go

Belinda Grimaudo Grayburn

Ninety pounds.

I follow my friend, Annie, to the window seat in her kitchen and notice that her tights look baggy.

"You know, people complain about taking weight off—I can't seem to keep it on!" she says, only half-joking.

"I like your new wig though," I say.

"Thanks," she replies with a big grin. She adjusts her black Cleopatra-style hairdo as we sit in our regular spot by the window.

I pour the tea.

"What's that?" I ask, pointing to a book on the nearby table.

"Just some photo albums I've been going through," she says.

"May I?"

"Of course!"

I flip through old photos. "Oh my gosh, Annie, is this you? Look at you in those days! How old were you then?"

"Nineteen."

"Wow, gorgeous picture."

"Is that Mark?" I tilt my head back and laugh. "Nice brown polyester pants!" I turn the page. "Oh, your wedding photos! They're lovely."

"Yes, Mark chased me for a long time."

"Really, you didn't want to get married?"

"Are you kidding? I was having too much fun. Mark was so serious and jealous and I was the complete opposite—a free spirit. He finally wore me down, though, and I got him to lighten up." She chuckles.

"How's he doing now?" I ask.

"Good. He comes to every appointment with me, works from home when he can, and takes on more of the household chores. Once my chemo's done, we plan to go to Cuba."

Eighty-one pounds.

I walk to the backyard deck and find Annie sitting in a chair. Wrapped in a blanket, she stares at the ground in front of her.

"Hi," I say and take a seat beside her. "How do you feel?"

"Toxic."

Mark opens the back door and joins us on the deck.

"Annie tolerated the first few rounds of chemo well," he says. "But this one hit her hard. We just need to make sure she stays hydrated."

"Let me make some tea," I offer and head back into the house.

Waiting for the water to boil, I notice the framed photos on the walls—vacations with their two boys, celebrations with family and friends, and international students who stayed in their home over the years.

Seventy-six pounds.

Annie and I sit together at the window seat in the kitchen. The radiation treatments to her neck have made it hard for her to speak.

"He did it again," she says coldly.

"Did what?"

"He cheated—and with the same woman!"

Annie pounds her fist against her bony leg.

"Why would he do this to me now? How could I be such an idiot? I feel like a fool—like it was happening all along and I was too stupid to notice."

"Are you sure he cheated?" I ask.

She nods. "I found e-mails." She takes off her glasses and wipes her dripping nose. "Why couldn't he just wait until I was gone?"

A year ago, Annie told me about Mark's first indiscretion.

"I was diagnosed in '94 and three years later, when I was in remission, he had an affair with a woman from work. I found out and kicked him out for nine months."

"What about the boys?" I inquired.

"I raised John and Eddie on my own and didn't tell anyone we separated. We showed up at functions together and then he went to his apartment and I went home at the end of the night."

"Did you want him back?"

"I wasn't sure. This didn't happen to couples like us, or at least, that's what I thought. In recovery, I talked with support groups and read articles only to find out that it was common."

"What do you mean?"

"Mark spent so much time caring for me and worrying about death, that once I was well, he looked for someone who was willing to take care of him, if only for a brief moment. So, after nine months of separation, I took him back."

"That's a hard one to forgive," I said.

"Sometimes, Belinda, good men do bad things."

Sixty-three pounds.

Annie can no longer speak. Mark bought a Magna Doodle for her to write on. This time, she has not kicked him out.

"How is it today?" I ask.

Annie writes:

Life is beautiful.
Death is peaceful.
Dying is hard.

Fifty-eight pounds.

Annie can no longer walk. Mark carries her from room to room and does his best to make her feel comfortable.

"Her lungs are filling with fluid and she can barely swallow. She's slowly suffocating and starving to death," Mark explains in a quiet but steady voice. "People will be here soon."

Annie's sister, Sandra, calls from upstairs. "Belinda, would you help me give Annie a sponge bath?"

"Sure, I'll be right there." I pat Mark's arm and walk upstairs.

To keep Annie warm, we uncover only small parts of her body at a given time—a foot, a leg, an arm.

So thin, I've never seen anyone so thin, I think to myself.

"Okay, Annie. We need to roll you over now," Sandra says.

Annie nods and braces for us to move her.

We turn her slowly until she lies on her belly. Three large lumps on her back stare up at us. Sandra and I freeze and look at each other. With chin and hands trembling, Sandra carefully cleans around her sister's tumours.

Fifty-four pounds.

"Annie wants to remain at home," Mark informs the visitors who crowd the main floor of their house.

I look at the line of people waiting to say goodbye. I walk past and recognize many of them. I nod at Annie's coworkers, Christine and George. I say hello to her neighbours, Mr. Murphy and his wife. I hug Annie's sister-in-law, Catherine, and her kids. I shake hands with Annie's old and dear friend, Susan, and wave to John and Mary, who Annie met in line at the grocery store only a few years ago. Annie's two boys, John and Eddie, sit with their grandparents in the family room.

I wait until later in the evening to see Annie. I enter her bedroom and find the hospice nurse swabbing morphine onto Annie's gums. I lie down on the bed beside Annie and wait for her to recognize me. Her eyes, dark and distant, eventually find my face.

"Hi," I say. I smile and cry at the same time.

She manages a smile and squeezes my hand as best she can. She opens her mouth to say something. I put my ear near her mouth to hear.

"Mark," she breathes softly.

"Okay, I'll get him."

Mark stays in the bedroom with Annie for the rest of the night. He reads her Robert Frost poems and he's by her side when she dies.

~~~

One year later, Mark marries the other woman.

Arnie's Closet

Robert Grant Price

What do you say to another man when you're sitting with him inside his closet? What constitutes appropriate small talk? I set the matter aside and talk to Arnie about the Internet.

He listens to me patiently.

The company I work for has designed a website for Life Rattle, the radio program and publishing house Arnie cofounded. When he invites me upstairs, I don't expect Arnie's office to be wedged into the closet of his bedroom.

The small chair pinches my bum. I have no room to stretch out my legs. The closet fits two men uncomfortably. Arnie does us both a favour and leaves the door open.

I walk Arnie through the commands that will give him access to the sparkling new Life Rattle website. I dictate the key strokes that will upload new content to the server. I show him how to write new headlines for the homepage. The company I work for has developed a solution that makes updating a website a brainless activity.

Arnie admits that the technology confuses him. "I prefer books. They're easier to use," he jokes.

We work for about half an hour. The only interruption is Sally, Arnie's Newfoundlander. She sticks her huge head into the closet and slobbers on Arnie's lap.

"Get out," Arnie says and closes the closet door.

The more I explain, the less sense the website makes. I grow confused. I feel like I am wasting Arnie's time. I worry he'll tell me I am wasting his time. I start over from the beginning.

"Okay. Now this is all very simple. We've set up a database that manages the content through a series of preset templates. The colours, the graphics; they're all set. The textual content is different. That's what you'll be changing."

Arnie glances at me. He looks frustrated. We are both frustrated. Arnie clears his throat. "Okay," he says, unconvinced.

We toy around with user functions, adding text to the site and watching it magically appear on the screen. Arnie gets tired of working on the site—I get tired of working on the site—so we leave his closet and go downstairs.

As I prepare to leave, we stand beside the stainless steel countertop that divides the kitchen from the living room and Arnie says to me, "The way you can change the content on the site, it's like changing the curtains inside a house—nothing changes except the colour of the curtains, right? That's all we're doing with that website."

"Yes," I say. What he says makes more sense than what I have been telling him.

Arnie pats Sally's back.

"That website is like a mansion," he finally says. "I think all Life Rattle needs is a cottage."

Or perhaps a closet, I think.

Chapter 6: Places

Write about a place.
Present details of incidents, people, setting and
landscape to show the character of the place.

The Elevator

Bayan Khatib

E ven with the darkness of the night and the gentle rocking of the van as my uncle drives, even with my head on Nana's warm lap, I can't fall asleep.

"Only a few more minutes," my uncle calls out.

In only a few minutes I will meet my parents for the first time since I was a baby. I have lived with my grandparents for the past seven years. It has taken Grandfather seven years to find a way to reunite me with my parents in America.

A few weeks ago Nana, the only mother I have known, told me that she is not my mother—she's my grandmother.

"This is your mother, your father, your brother and your sisters," she said as she showed me pictures. "Your mother is very nice and she's going to take very good care of you."

It felt like Nana was telling me an imaginary story.

My grandparents and I flew to Mississippi, where my eldest uncle lives. As soon as my uncle got a break from work, we started driving to Denver, Colorado, where my real family lives.

After hours and hours of driving, my uncle finally says, "We're here." He parks the van in front of an old brown building. A man and a woman run down the stairs from an upstairs apartment.

"That's them," my uncle says.

Someone lifts me off the ground into a tight embrace. I feel kisses all over my face. Tears stream down the cheeks of the woman who holds me so tightly. The man beside her takes me from her and hugs me and kisses me and carries me up the stairs into a small apartment.

"The kids fell asleep," my mother says, as if she were apologizing. "They tried hard to stay awake, but it got too late. They were really excited to meet their new sister."

"I'll go wake them up," my father says.

"They can wait till tomorrow."

But my father is already in the bedroom. Seconds later, three wide-awake children, ages three, four and five, walk out and sit next to my mother on the floor. My father introduces us to each other. None of us say anything. We stare at each other as the adults speak.

I sleep on the floor and Nana cuddles me as she does every night. I will soon have to learn how to sleep without Nana's arms around me.

At the beginning, my brother wants to give me all his toys. At the beginning, I think being a big sister might be fun.

After a few weeks, everything changes.

One morning, my brother tells me that he wants to show me something in the building across the street. I love adventure. My brother and I run to the building. We walk through the dim, empty entrance.

"Do you know what that is?" my brother asks.

"No."

"It's an elevator."

"What's an elevator?"

"Come, I'll show you."

My brother presses the "UP" button. The elevator door opens and we walk in together. He presses 20, the highest number on the side panel. Just before the door closes completely, my brother runs out of the elevator. I stand alone. The door shuts and the elevator starts to move. I push and hit the door. It won't open. I watch the numbers light up on the panel—3, 4, 5, 6, 7—until it finally reaches 20.

The door opens and I run out. I look around. I see nothing. I hear nothing. I feel scared. I sit on the floor in front of the elevator and cry and cry and cry. I think about Nana and cry. I think about my home in Syria and cry. I think about my new family and cry.

A woman with two children walks to the elevator and presses the "DOWN" button. She looks at me. I look at her. She asks me questions that I don't understand.

"I don't speak English," I say in Arabic.

"You speak Arabic?"

"Yes."

"Why are you crying?"

"I don't know how to go back home."

"Where do you live?"

"I don't know."

"What's your mother's name?"

I don't know what to answer. I want to tell her Nana's name, but I know she wouldn't know Nana. She might know Mama.

"Do you know a woman named Dawn?"

"Yes," the woman replies. "She's my friend. She lives in the building across from here. Oh my God, are you Dawn's daughter, the one who just came from Syria?"

"Yes."

"Come with me. I'll take you to her."

Nana taught me to never go anywhere with a stranger, but this woman seems my only hope of ever getting back to Nana. I follow the lady back to my parents' apartment. My mother hugs me as she thanks her friend over and over.

I tell my mother what my brother did to me. He runs to his room. Mama runs after him and shuts my brother's door behind her. I hear her yell. I hear him scream. I feel nothing for him.

~~~

The next morning, my father takes me back to the building and teaches me how to use an elevator.

Cellphone

Peter Palladini

I'm not happy with just a pager, so I bother my parents for a cellphone. But I don't want just any cellphone. I want a Motorola flip phone. My mother doesn't like the idea of her fifteen-year-old son having a pager, let alone a cellphone, and I know there's going to be some yelling, arguing, kissing ass and making up. At the end of it all, as usual, I get my way.

Even though I hang out with all my friends at the same pool hall every night, I must have a cellphone. It isn't that I need the phone, but I like how other people—mainly girls—treat you when they see that you have one. It makes me feel important, respected, looked up to, and most of all, wealthy.

At school, I wear my phone on one side of my belt and my pager on the other. The school doesn't allow pagers or cellphones because they disrupt class, but I don't care. I have an image to uphold.

I met a girl, about a month ago, I'm quite fond of. Her name is Mary. My best friend John dates Mary's best friend, Diane, and since I don't have the courage to ask Mary out, I asked John to do it for me.

John is on his way to meet Diane and Mary downtown and he's gonna ask Mary if it would be okay for me to join them. John said he's gonna call me on my cellphone at eight-thirty sharp to let me know the answer.

I get all dressed up in a pair of my least-faded black jeans and a black T-shirt that I had to pull out of the hamper. I run out of the house as fast as I can. I sit in Coffee Time Donuts and wait for John's call. It's eight-twenty. If John gives me the okay, I'll take the bus downtown.

I'm getting nervous. What if she says no? My right hand rests on my cellphone while my left hand fidgets with my lighter. My palms sweat. My throat is dry. I take a sip of cold coffee. I eye my phone. I check the time—eight-twenty-eight. He's not gonna call. She said no. He can't bring himself to tell me the bad news. I tell myself I won't take it that bad. It won't be the end of the world.

I look around me. The coffee shop is empty except for a man and a woman sitting at a table in the corner playing cards. They seem in another world. Their eyes don't rise above their cards. They remain focussed on their cards, their strategy, their lives. The clerk at the counter scratches her head as she reads the newspaper. They don't care that I'm waiting for an important call.

Ring. Ring. Ring.

It's him. It's John. I knew he'd call. My heart pounds. My hands shake. What will he say?

"Hello. Mom? Wha'd'ya want? No, I'm not being rude. I'm just waiting for an important call. Okay, okay, I won't be home late to-night. Yes, Mom, I promise. Yes, Mom. I love you, too. Okay, bye."

Shit. John's not gonna call. What if he called when I was on the phone with Mom? He better try again if he got a busy signal. Mom can't leave me alone for one second. If John doesn't call, it's all her fault.

A customer enters. My eyes follow his sluggish, clumsy feet as he drags his body every step of the way. His worn, faded blue jeans are splattered with stains of what looks like dry blood. His grey hair is oily. His beard, uneven, untrimmed and uncombed, reaches halfway down his chest. I can smell the stench of his body from across the coffee shop.

He methodically walks past the lady at the counter, who continues to read her paper, and makes his way to the bathroom door. He takes a brief look over his shoulder at the lady and then sets his eyes on me. My face flushes. I look away. He disappears into the washroom.

Ring. Ring. Ring.

I jump out of my seat. I almost forgot that I'm waiting for John to call.

"Hello, Ma. I told you I was waiting for a call. No. No. Bye!"

I can't believe Mom. She never leaves me alone.

I stare at the clock—eight-forty-two.

What happened to the guy in the washroom? I wonder who's winning at cards. I feel my eyes burn. I want to scream. My back tenses and my hands are cold and clammy. I don't even like Mary that much. I don't know why I'm making such a big deal out of this anyway.

Ring. Ring. Ring.

"Hello John! Why didn't you call earlier? Yeah, I've been waiting at the Coffee Time. Well, what's the story? Good news and bad news? Tell me the good news first. Hello? Hello? John? Can you hear me? My battery's dying. What? I can't hear you. All I hear is static. John? John?"

My battery dies. John had called from a payphone. He's not calling back. I light a cigarette. I think about my wasted night.

I take another look around. The couple still plays cards in the corner, the clerk still reads her newspaper and the man with the beard is still in the washroom.

St. Laurent

Vincent Gao

"**B**onne weekend, Vincent," says Gaëtan, my sixty-two-year-old supervisor.

"*Et vous aussi* (And you too)," I respond with one of the few French phrases I know.

I step out of Centre Pauline-Charron, a francophone seniors' centre in Vanier, the sketchiest neighbourhood in Ottawa. A gust of cold November wind punches me in the gut and bites me in the face. I zip up my jacket and start towards the bus stop on McArthur Avenue. I pass by pawnshops, porn shops and payday loan centres.

Fifteen minutes later, the red and white bus arrives and I hop on. The bus takes me up the avenue and back to the main station at the St. Laurent Shopping Centre. Neon lights glow against the darkening sky. I walk down the stairs to the terminal. Fluorescent lights flicker against the naked concrete walls. Shoppers chat with bags in hand, a few government workers pace around in their suits, a businessman checks his watch. Red and white buses flow in and out, but there's no number 27 bus to Orléans.

I find an empty spot on the platform. I stretch and yawn and scratch my nose. My hand smells like ham. Today I helped Gaëtan prepare ham and gravy for the banquet this weekend. I'm glad I won't be working the banquet. I'm not a senior citizen. I don't speak French. I wouldn't fit in. On my first day at the seniors' centre, Gaëtan greeted me and then introduced me to my coworkers in

Quebecoise French. I smiled and nodded until he realized I didn't speak French and switched to English.

A lady in a big grey winter coat asks me for the time. I don't wear a watch or carry a cellphone. "Sorry, I don't know," I tell her. She wanders off.

I watch the red and white buses pull in and out of the grey terminal. I watch people come and go. I wonder about the people in my life. I wonder about Sophie and Joseph cooking for us and taking care of the house this week and Jay and Megan volunteering at the food bank and Kate working at the museum and Kamille at the drug prevention facility and Marie-André at the daycare and Sally and Ben and Alexe helping out at the elementary school.

I wonder if they made it home yet.

I wonder about my friends in the mechanical engineering program I dropped out of at the University of Toronto and about my mother at home in Hamilton and about my father away on a business trip in China and about my ex-girlfriend graduating from university.

I push them out of my mind.

Another bus pulls into the station—not the one I want.

I wonder some more.

Clancy's

Tyler Mclaren

We sit with our butts in the back of my Ford Explorer. The trailer hitch sticks out between our feet. The trunk door blocks our view of the sky and keeps the snow out of our hair. Hannah rests her head on my shoulder. We kiss, drink Alexander Keith's, and talk about her family. She wants to move out. I tell her not to be dramatic. She shivers and her teeth chatter. I take her hands in mine and rub them together. She complains about my calluses. In my best Clint Eastwood voice, I tell her that hand cream is for pussies. She laughs and runs her hand through my hair. I drive her home. Hannah says she'll text me tomorrow.

~~~

My boxing gloves stink of sweat and feet and vinegar. I shower them in peach-scented Febreze and toss them in my gym bag along with wraps and a jump rope. I trudge toward a giant black banner that reads "Clancy's Boxing Academy." A bright green clover substitutes for the apostrophe. I swallow bottled water and check my cellphone.

I pull open the door and stomp my shoes against the floor. Clumps of snow fall from my feet onto the floor mat. I nod to Coach who sits with his laptop open. His eight-year-old son, Andre, bounces on his knee. Andre waves excitedly at my arrival. He smiles and I see gaps where teeth have fallen out.

"Hi, Tyler!"

"Hi, Andre. Did you go see *Iron Man 2?*"

"Yeah! It was so cool!"

"That's good, buddy."

"Tyler, go warm up." Coach keeps a hand on Andre's shoulder so that he stays put. "We'll hit the pads."

"Yeah, Coach. Don't spend all day on the shitter this time," I say with a grin. He laughs. I check my phone again. Nothing.

I wrap my hands, weaving between my fingers and over my knuckles. I clench them a few times. I check my phone, then start jumping rope. I alternate feet with every jump. Posters of "The Greats"—Muhammad Ali, Roy Jones Jr., Floyd Mayweather Jr., Bernard Hopkins—cover the walls. Each one has a quote that says something about hard work or perseverance.

I see Justin, and Arthur, the new guy, who wants to learn to fight better for hockey. Justin hits the heavy bag. Arthur swings a sledge-hammer against an old tire in the corner. He should be working on his punching technique. "Fuckin' hockey players," I grumble. I trip on my rope and start over. I trip again after just a few jumps. I check my phone. I step up to the ring, lift one rope, and duck underneath. I shadowbox a little, but I feel stiff and off-balance.

"Tyler, you're gonna move around with Arthur for a few." Coach points Arthur toward the headgear.

"Coach, can you just have him spar with Justin? I feel like shit."

"C'mon, bro!" Arthur chimes in. "Thought you were a fighter!" He claps his gloved hands together loudly and smirks.

Fuckin' hockey players.

Coach tells Justin to get in the ring. I jump out.

Bwop. Bwop. Hannah's number has a special notification. The sound of water drops means a text from her. I read it.

"I don't know what to say about yesterday…but I can't do this now. Sorry."

My sweat smears the screen. I decide to fight Arthur.

I pop in my mouth guard and pace in my corner. Arthur stares at me from across the ring, chest puffed out. The buzzer sounds. Coach shouts, "Box!"

I keep my guard tight over my head and hunch to protect my midsection. Arthur stands upright, his hands down. I circle around the ring, leading with my right foot. Arthur plods forward. He swings big, hard, awkward hooks. I absorb his shots, tremors running through my forearms. He lands a hook to my cheekbone. He laughs and nods his head. Coach shouts at me to "throw back." I do. I land one on Arthur's temple. He groans and puts his hands on his knees to stay up. Coach tells him he's done for the day.

I mutter an apology nobody hears. I pack my gloves, wraps and jump rope, and head back out into the snow.

I don't check my phone.

An Unexpected Afternoon

Samir Toma

May 2001, Mosul, Iraq

I sit in the middle seat of the front row in grade seven at Al Nour Secondary School. My shirt clings to my body from the sweltering afternoon heat and humidity. Students remain quiet as Ms. Hiba, our history teacher, writes on the chalkboard.

Principal Sharif's voice breaks the silence. We look at each other. Something major must have happened for the principal to interrupt the last period.

Ms. Hiba instructs everyone to leave the room. We rush out into the wide hallway. Ms. Hiba lines us up, then motions for us to go outside into the schoolyard. The entire student body, from grade seven to grade nine, stands in silence.

An Iraqi army general, wearing a black beret and a side arm pistol, stomps onto the playground. Twelve soldiers flank him. The general glares at everyone over his well-trimmed, black moustache. Four soldiers set down a grey plastic table in front of us. My gaze lingers over the black stains, scratch marks and cracks that mark the surface. A soldier hands the general an assault rifle. He grips the rifle's handle, sets it on the table, and begins to take the weapon apart.

"This is the firing pin." The general's voice booms. "This is the chamber and piston."

I do not know why he tells all this information to elementary school students.

The general finishes his lecture about the gun parts. He surveys the crowd and picks up a gun part from the table. "What is this part called?" he asks.

I stand in the forty-five degree heat, sweat dripping down my forehead. He looks towards me, points and shouts, "You there, in the back row, what is this part called?"

I hold my breath. My knees shake.

"The gas chamber, sir!" shouts a student.

I close my eyes and slowly exhale.

They divide us into groups of ten, each under the direction of a general. An old general, with wrinkles lining his face, approaches my group. "Drop down and give me a hundred pushups!"

As we move to follow his command, my friend Saif turns his head to me and whispers, "How the hell are we supposed to do a hundred pushups?"

"Shut up before he sees us talking," I whisper back.

The general squints at Saif and me. "You, in the grey shirt, come here!" I look at my clothes and realize I'm not the one wearing the grey shirt.

Saif stands up on trembling legs. He trudges towards the general. I keep an eye on Saif as I do my pushups.

"Drop on the ground, now!" yells the general. Saif does as he's told. "Start rolling on the ground, now!"

Saif rolls on the sandy schoolyard all the way to the fence and back. Gravel sticks to his face, sand clings to his hair and small stones stick to his ripped shirt.

"AGAIN!" orders the general.

Saif rolls again. He rolls and rolls and rolls. Then Saif stands up in front of everyone, face bruised.

"I hope you have learned your lesson," the general says.

Saif puts his head down and walks back to our group.

The day continues with more punishments, more pushups, more lectures on how to use assault rifles. We stand in confusion, wondering why we are being taught these things.

The school day comes to an end at 3:45 p.m. The general with the black moustache, hands clasped behind him, paces back and forth in front of us.

"Iraq is going to war. You are the future soldiers that must defend your country," he says. "You must give your lives for your beloved Iraq if needed to do so."

I run home. I walk into the house and see Dad. I tell him what happened. Dad looks worried but not surprised.

Sinan, my older brother who is in fourth-year university, comes home and tells me the same thing happened to him. My sister Sandra, in her second year at Mosul University, and my other brother Sal, in grade nine, recount the same story.

~~~

Six months later, Dad secretly sells our house. We leave Iraq for Syria.

Calf Bully

Christie Rodenburg

I stomp my black rubber boots and step up into the milking parlour, in the old section of the barn of our family farm in Corinth, Ontario. I stand between two metal pipes above the stairs to the pit and tug on the belt loops of my faded jeans. I watch Dad attach a milker to a sagging Jersey udder.

He turns and grins. "Hi, Christie."

"Hey." I pass down a black and a white pail.

Dad balances a wide, shiny milk can in his calloused hand and fills each pail halfway. "Michael picked up two heifers for the mega hut from Reuben today. They can't drink out of a pail, so you get to help them. Look for Number 43," he flops the lid back onto the milk can, "and 46."

"Okay."

The mega hut, a large white plastic structure surrounded by a lopsided rectangle of mismatched gates, sits to the right of our short row of calf hutches. I drag my boots through the gravel. Two calves rush to the fence. I check their white ear tags—43 and 46. *Perfect.* I set the white pail down and in one motion lift the black pail and my leg over the wire gate. My pants stretch at the crotch as I swing my other leg over.

Number 46, a Holstein with two black speckles on her nose, nudges me. I place two fingers in her mouth and push her nose into the pail. Her teeth dig into my fingers, but she drinks without spilling much. When she finishes, I toss the empty pail over the fence and lift the half-full white one. The contented heifer head-butts me and slides her raspy tongue along my arm and my shit-stained soccer camp T-shirt.

The other calf I have to feed, number 43, has more black markings on her forehead. As I approach her, she bolts into the mega hut. She fidgets on the opposite side of a faded green manger. I shuffle through the straw towards her. Her hooves thud and scrabble against the mega hut's wall and she skedaddles back outside.

This one's a real winner. I follow her outside. I catch her and thrust my body against her, pressing the calf into the side of a rusty gate. I start lifting the pail up to her nose. It wobbles in my hand. The heifer jerks her head upward and the pail's metal handle pinches my fingers. The other calf nuzzles my side. Strings of slobber stick to my T-shirt.

"Euuch!"

I remove my soggy hand from the calf's chin and lift the pail high. I spring over the fence, set the pail in the grass and jog across the gravel into the feed room. I peer around the mixer. My brother Andrew closes the hanging door to the high-moisture corn silo. I shout over the sound of conveyors, "Hey bud, can you do me a favour?"

"One sec," he calls back.

I tread around the dusty mixer. "One stupid calf won't drink and the other one's all over me. I think she's still hungry. Can you hold her off while I try to get some milk into Stupid?"

"Alright."

Andrew turns the conveyors and mixer off and follows me out through the garage door. We hop the gate. Andrew plants himself in front of the speckled heifer. I straddle Stupid. I dig my knees into her furry neck and force her face into the pail. She jerks wildly. She doesn't drink. I push my body down on her neck and wrap one arm around her head. I poke and massage her throat. The milk bubbles. She doesn't swallow.

Fucker, I think. I never say that word out loud.

Milk slops out of the pail. My wrist bends too far. *It's for your own good, dumbass. You need to drink!* I lower the pail as she gasps for air.

"Wow," Andrew says as he pushes his calf away from the milk in my pail.

I thrust Stupid's muzzle into the pail again. Five seconds later, I let up. She bucks her head and kicks her legs. I stop trying to sit on her and let her run. The calf Andrew held back clambers to join Stupid behind the mega hut.

"What a dumbass," I say. Large splotches of milk darken my jeans.

"She won't suck on your fingers?" Andrew asks.

"I spend all my time forcing her head into the pail. I don't have enough hands to get her to suck on my fingers too." I wipe my slippery hand on my T-shirt.

I nod to Andrew and we sneak around the mega hut. Stupid runs. I shout at her, "Don't you want to drink?"

Again, I push her against a fence and lock my knees around her neck. She twitches her head and my fingers slip along her slimy muzzle. Black and white hairs rub off her face and into the milk.

"I really just want to dump all the milk on her head!" I drop the pail into the dirt.

"Don't waste it," Andrew says.

I look down at the half-full pail. "My back hurts."

"Let's go. This is a waste of time."

"Okay." I stand up and stretch my arms. "I was totally wrestling her. That is not how this usually goes."

We hop the gate. I pick up the empty black pail I tossed over the fence earlier. I inhale a shocked laugh.

"I think she's scared of me now."

The Back Stairwell

Saamiyah Ali-Mohammed

*The whole earth is a masjid (place for prayer) and pure,
the Prophet Muhammad said.*

F rigid winter wind seeps in through the doorway and ruffles
my purple crepe headscarf. Icy mist frosts the floor-to-ceiling
window. I pray for the first time in the back stairwell of the Davis
Building at the University of Toronto Mississauga.

A fleece glove lies abandoned on the windowsill. A fly smacks
into the window and buzzes down the glass. My toes curl on the
cement. Professor Khan's voice squawks over a microphone in the
adjoining lecture hall. He answers students' questions during the
ten-minute break, too short a break to walk to the prayer room.

A door opens and voices echo in the stairwell above me. The door
whooshes shut. Boots clunk on the stairs. The door that leads into
the lecture hall thuds open against the concrete wall.

"Bipolar involves both depressive and manic episodes," Professor
Khan says. "On the other hand, depression—"

The door swings closed and muffles Professor Khan's voice.

I stand in *qiyām*. I learned at age three to fold my right hand over
my left hand and then place them both on my chest. I learned to fix
my eyes on the floor and memorized verses from the Qu'rān.

Qiyām. Standing for the recitation of
al-Fātiḥah and other verses of the Qur'ān

I look down, rest my hands on my chest and whisper verses into the silence.

> 37. *[Abraham said] "O our Lord! I have made some of my offspring to dwell in an uncultivable valley by Your Sacred House (Ka'bah), so that they may perform prayer...*
>
> 40. *"O my Lord, make me and my offspring among those who perform prayer. And accept my invocation."*

I bow down in *rukū'* and splay my fingers over my knees. I keep my back straight while I bow and after I rise.

 Rukū': Bowing at the waist

I crouch in *sujūd* and the grain of the concrete floor digs into my forehead. In Arabic, *sujūd* means "to submit." In prayer, *sujūd* refers to prostration and the placement of seven body parts on the floor: the forehead (including the nose), both hands, both knees and the bottoms of the toes of both feet. Sujūd symbolizes complete submission to God in all aspects of life.

 Sujūd: Prostration

I sit up and then prostrate again. The Prophet Muhammad sometimes recited verses aloud in qiyām. His companions, tribal leaders and *jinns* (spiritual beings) stopped to listen.

When in sujūd, he only whispered.

The wind whistles. A toilet flushes in the women's washroom across the hall. My eyelids droop. I mouth the words.

The door at the top of the staircase swings open and rattles against the wall. Dust puffs up like talcum powder. A guy and a girl walk down the stairs. Coffee sloshes onto the steps. The guy giggles, steps onto the landing and stops mid-giggle.

My heart beats faster. The floor bites into my knees. I hiss my praise of God.

I jump up, crack my knuckles and murmur under my breath. My lips fumble and I mispronounce all the Arabic words.

1. Say: He is Allah, the one and only

2. Allah, the eternal, absolute

3. He begetteth not nor is He begotten.

4. And there is none like unto Him.

I stare at the replica of the *Ka'bah* (Muslim house of worship in Mecca) woven into the top of my dark blue *sajjadah,* a prayer mat that Muslims orient to face the Ka'bah before we begin prayer. My sneakers sit at its edge.

I rock on the balls of my bare feet.

The girl's heeled boots click and the boy's sneakers squelch in a musical beat as they pass. "Come on," she says. The door behind me creaks open and bangs closed. The clicks fade as they walk down the hallway.

I bow down, straighten, and fall into sujūd. My glasses clack against the concrete. I sit back on my heels, praise the Prophet, then mutter, *"Assalamu alaikum* (Peace be upon you)." The angels greeted the first man and prophet, Prophet Adam, with these words. Muslims greet each other with these words. We also say *assalamu alaikum* to the angels, and to the worshippers left and right of us to signify the end of the prayer.

A blonde hair clings to the hem of my sajjadah. I brush off the hair, fold my sajjadah into a rectangle and tuck it into my coat pocket. I yank on my running shoes, run up the stairs and duck into class.

"Where were you?" asks Amanjit as I slide back into the seat next to her.

"I bought a coffee," I say.

Amanjit frowns. "I was there."

"I was…I was praying, actually," I say.

"Oh," she says. "You could have just said so."

Campfire

Anne Yendell

Forty *gaijin* (non-Japanese) girls and their parents assemble on the pavement in front of Tokyo's Azabu-Jūban Station. Rush-hour commuters stare and dodge between us to reach the subway entrance. We stand in groups with backpacks, sleeping bags and canteens at our sides, chattering at a pitch higher than the noise of the traffic, street vendors and the audible crossing signal for the blind. A small blue flag darts through the air above us.

Mrs. Yamaguchi, our troop leader, lowers the flag and blows her whistle. Chaperones direct us toward the sliding glass doors. Parents wave as our troop shadows the stream of commuters down into the station.

Mrs. Yamaguchi, a former Girl Guide, hails from Atlanta, Georgia. She speaks rapid Japanese with a southern accent to the white-gloved official in the ticket booth. They bow to each other from either side of the kiosk glass. Mrs. Yamaguchi raises her blue flag and we scramble to keep pace as we follow it down to our platform. Tickets clasped in French manicured hands, scout whistle clamped between red-lipsticked lips and shoulders cast back, Mrs. Yamaguchi marshals us up the carriage steps.

In the abrupt hush of the spotless, air-conditioned compartment, we clamber for seats and then stow our backpacks overhead. We share Japanese tangerines, called *mecons*, and deliberate the merits of the badges we aspire to earn. After several stops, Mrs. Yamaguchi abandons her seat and advances down the cabin aisle. The whistle bounces against her prominent chest with every step she takes.

"Girls, hush! Now pay attention. We change trains at the very next station," she announces from the front of the carriage. "Please put on your packs and wait by the doors."

We disembark and stand two by two on the platform. Sickening smells of soba, sweat and urine hang in the air. Mrs. Yamaguchi counts heads and stands at the front of the line. The blue flag leads us up a set of stairs, across a bridge and then back down again to the next train. My friends chat about sleeping outside. I find it difficult to keep up with them.

In front of the train on the Tohoku Shinkansen Line, we fall in formation and wait for Mrs. Yamaguchi's inspection. She glances at me and then halts.

"You look pasty, Anne-chan." She lays the back of her cool hand on my forehead. "Young lady, you have quite a fever."

Mrs. Yamaguchi removes me from the line. She waves my friends aboard and grips my arm as we climb the steps onto the train. She helps me pull off my pack and sits me between her and her daughter, Keiko. I peer at my friends across the aisle. Their voices fade as I press my burning cheek against the linen-covered headrest. I feel the rhythmic vibration of steel wheels against steel rails and float into a tangled sleep.

Keiko's finger taps my shoulder. I respond slowly, disoriented by the abrupt transition from city concrete to country woodlands as the train slowly pulls into the station. Mrs. Yamaguchi stands, flag in hand, in the aisle. Her index finger points out the gum and candy wrappers, mecon peels, pop cans, teen magazines and tissues that litter our seats. Her eyes dart along the compartment floor, looking for canteens, snacks, books and playing cards that belong in our packs.

The train comes to a halt and we step onto the platform. The elevated blue flag signals the resumption of our hike. We trek forward into the forest. Cicadas announce the reemergence of the sun from behind a column of clouds. The skin of my hands, lips and eyes feels stung and swollen.

We arrive at the campground entrance. A ranger emerges from the office. He salutes. Mrs. Yamaguchi's heels snap. They confer, nod, and suck their teeth. Rivulets of sweat run down my spine and make my T-shirt stick to my back. Mrs. Yamaguchi and the ranger bow repeatedly, signalling the end of their exchange. She raises the blue flag and marches us into the park.

The campsite comes into view. My friends flit excitedly from one tent to the next, staking their claims with their sleeping bags. A chaperone leads me to her tent. I rest my head against my pack while she fishes for a thermometer in the first aid kit. She takes my temperature, shakes her head, and leaves the tent. I fall asleep.

Hours later, I am startled awake by Mrs. Yamaguchi. Her face glows, distorted and mask-like, above the beam of her flashlight.

"As I'm sure you realize, Anne-chan, this is all very inconvenient. With the ranger's assistance, I have contacted your parents and they will arrive sometime during the evening to take you home."

"Please, Mrs. Yamaguchi. I'm feeling much better—really," I assure her. "If I go home now, how can I possibly collect the merit badges for this nature unit?"

Mrs. Yamaguchi smiles her masquerade smile and leaves. My friends sing Scout songs. The campfire blazes. My eyes burn.

Someone touches my hand.

Keiko kneels beside me. She strokes the hot skin of my forearm as she stares out through the tent flaps at the girls sitting in the campfire circle. She shakes her head and whispers, "I'd love to go back home."

On The Bus

Rahul Sethi

A ton of black kids with mean mugs pack the bleachers at Clarkson Secondary School. They boo and throw empty pop cans as we walk into the gym.

"I don't think they like us," I say.

Mike grins. "Nah, man. I fit right in. I bet you half these niggas is either related to me or go to my church. It's *you* they don't like. A paki in a nigga's school." Mike chuckles, then knocks the basketball loose from my hands. "And a basketball-playing paki at that."

Clarkson's principal, a tall man with thick arms, yells at the students in the bleachers. He orders them to pick the cans up off the floor.

"Shit, what I just say?" Mike points at a cute girl in baggy jeans and a long sweatshirt. She waves at Mike from the bleachers. "That's my cousin Sheila and her friends right there."

A group of girls with tight braids and colourful weaves sit around Sheila. Mike smiles. "I be right back."

Clarkson students glare at Mike as his lanky legs jog toward the bleachers. Guys stand and cross their arms. They sit back down as Mike leans in and hugs Sheila.

I pick up the basketball and dribble to our bench.

I've known Mike since grade seven. His parents split a year before he and his mom, Ms. Williams, moved from Jane and Finch to a block away from where I live at Dundas and Highway 10—or 5 and 10 as we call it—in Mississauga. Ms. Williams works as a librarian. She makes Mike read at least two new books each month, on top of his schoolwork. He even has to discuss the books with his mom when he's done. Only I know this.

Our midget team plays first. The junior team plays after us. It's just an exhibition game but Mr. Clark tells us to *treat it like it counts.*

"The first game sets the trend for the rest of the season, boys," he says. "So no friggin' around!"

The junior team sits at the empty end of the bleachers. They avoid the stark eyes of the Clarkson students and ignore the comments made about their mothers, and their sexual preferences. They sit huddled together, backpacks between their knees. The juniors are older than us, of course, but only a couple of them are taller than me and Mike. Mr. Clark says they all play like pussies. "They frig around too much," he scoffs.

Clarkson boos and curses every time one of our players touches the ball. Sheila and her friends cheer every time Mike gets a pass or makes a basket. When Mike doesn't have the ball, Sheila and her friends chant, "Pass it to Mike. Pass it to Mike. Pass it to Mike."

We pass it to Mike as much as possible, just to have someone cheering us on. Mike relishes it.

With ten seconds left in the game, we're up 54-52. Clarkson has possession at their end of the court and they have to inbound the ball. "Full court press!" Mr. Clark shouts.

Andre, Zorie, Mike and Tom hover over the Clarkson players. As the centre, I stand at half court and serve as the safety.

Clarkson's bench, our bench and the students in the bleachers stand to watch. My heart pounds under my jersey. No threes, I tell myself. Keep your hands up so that whatever fucker takes the shot can't see the net.

"Alright boys, tight D," Mr. Clark yells. "No friggin' around!"

The referee's whistle blows and Clarkson's players dodge all over the court to get open. Their point guard gets by Tom and catches a long toss down court. Mike rushes at the point guard and tries to sweep the ball away. The short point guard dribbles, ducks under Mike's lanky arm, and sprints by him. He charges in my direction. I hunch and move toward him. The point guard crosses the ball between his legs and jolts to the basket. I follow beside him until we're both under the net. I stretch my arms out further and leap as he jumps to shoot. "Foul 'im!" Mr. Clark shrieks from the bench.

I hack at the point guard's arm. *Smack.* The ball floats over the backboard and the point guard falls to the floor. The buzzer screams to signal the end of the game. The Clarkson student body roars.

The referee blows his whistle.

"Foul." He clasps his wrist and tells me to spin around. It's the last personal foul I have left. My hand throbs from the hack. The referee glances at the number on the back of my jersey. "Foul, on the shot, number three-zero." He holds up two fingers. "Two shots. No added time." The referee waves over the point guard.

The Clarkson student body simmers as the point guard limps over to the free-throw line. "Let's go, Damien," someone bellows from the bleachers.

Let's not, Damien, I think to myself.

I sit on our bench and sweat. My hands press together.

Damien dribbles at the free-throw line. The referee blows a gentle whistle. The gym falls silent as Damien stares at the net and gently bends his knees. He slowly lifts the ball past his waist, past his stomach, his chest, his shoulders, neck, face and head. He flicks his wrist as his arm straightens, sending the ball hurling towards the basket.

Swish.

"Shit!" I whip my towel.

Clarkson cheers and stomps their feet on the bleachers. Clarkson's coach nods his approval. I look at the scoreboard—54-53.

Mr. Clark clutches his clipboard to his chest.

Mike winks and waves at one of Sheila's friends. "I'll talk to you after the game," he mouths.

The referee tosses the ball to Damien. "Last shot. Alright coaches, if he makes this we go into overtime." He blows his whistle.

Damien stands at the free-throw line and dribbles. My heart pumps with every bounce of the ball on the glimmering court. Damien bends his knees. The gym falls silent again. Damien slowly lifts the ball past his waist, past his stomach, his chest, his shoulders, neck, face and head. He flicks his wrist as his arm straightens, sending the ball hurling towards the basket.

Clank. The ball springs off the rim and bounces back down court. Our bench howls and jumps.

"Friggin' A!" Mr. Clark shakes his fist and pats the shoulders of the players within his reach. "Good job, boys. A little closer than I'd like the game to be, but good job. Way to treat it like it counts. Good foul. Way to hit 'im, Raul."

Mike chuckles and pushes me. "Friggin' A, man," he snickers. "Friggin' A."

~~~

Our midget team sits inside the dark bus parked in front of Clarkson Secondary. We wait for the juniors to change into their street clothes and board. They lost 63-49.

Mike and I sit on the worn seats at the back of the bus and make cracks at Sheila's fat friend Shawntai.

"Yo, you see that girl's weave." Mike laughs. "Here she is tryin' to tell me she's half Spanish when it look like she got that hair fresh off a horse this mornin'." He chuckles. "And the girl can't catch a hint. I told her, like, five times that I ain't 'bout to give her my number."

I laugh.

Three large Clarkson students climb onto the bus. They scan the players in the seats. "Where dat tall Indian kid?" one of them bellows. His arms look too big for his sleeves.

"Where he at?" He stares at the blank faces of our team. "We just wanna talk to 'im."

Mike nudges me. I slouch into my seat.

The last time our team won an exhibition game at Clarkson, some of their students whipped a two-by-four at the bus and cracked the front windshield.

"Where the hell is Mr. Clark?" I whisper to Mike. "Where the hell is the bus driver?"

Mike stares straight ahead and shrugs.

"Shit," I whisper.

"Eh, look. We just lookin' for dat Indian kid. Dat was my lil' brother dat kid hit and now he got a twisted ankle. I just want 'im to say sorry, dat's it. Now where da fuck he at?"

Damien's brother walks down the bus aisle. His wide frame and bulky forearms rub along the outer edge of bus seats as he walks closer towards Mike and me.

Silence.

Mike elbows me and gestures for me to hide under the seat. I shift and slide. My knees bump the seat in front. I crouch near Mike's feet and try to slide under our seat but can't bend low enough.

I look up at Mike. "I can't fit," I whisper.

Mike waves a hand at me to shut up. "I think he's inside the school still, in the washroom or somethin'," Mike says. He pushes down on my head, trying to force me under the seat. My neck strains. I slap his hand away.

Damien's brother grins. "Fuck dat."

Mike hits me with the side of his knee.

"We know he ain't in da washroom." Footsteps approach our seat. "We saw da kid walk on da bus."

Mike pushes my head down and kicks me with the side of his foot. I squeeze to get under the seat but can't manage it.

"He ain't sittin' next to you, is he?" Damien's brother asks.

Shit. Shit. Shit. My legs, neck and back ache as I bend and arc against the seat. Mike throws his bag on my head and moves his legs closer to me. I hold my breath.

The footsteps stop. Damien's brother hovers over us.

"Like I said, he's in the washroom," Mike says.

Damien's brother lifts Mike out of his seat, picks up his backpack, and throws it at him. I look up from where I sit squashed on the floor. I smile awkwardly. He grabs me by the collar of my shirt and pulls me up.

"I'm sorry," I gasp.

Damien's brother laughs and yanks me to the front of the bus. The other two Clarkson students grab me by the arms and drag me to the door. I tug and jump and try to pull away. Everyone in the bus stands but only Mike tries to pull the guys off. Damien's brother grabs Mike by the throat and tosses him onto a seat. "Sit da fuck down, nigga. This ain't none of yo' business."

Mr. Clark steps onto the bus.

"What the frig is goin' on here? Let go of him right now!"

Mr. Clark pulls Damien's brother and the other two off me. "Get the hell off of my bus before I call your principal!" He points to the door.

Damien's brother doesn't move; he grips my collar tighter. Mr. Clark takes a step toward him. Damien's brother kisses his teeth, punches me in the gut, and shoves me into Mr. Clark. The three guys nudge Mr. Clark as they stride to the door, jump out of the bus, and take off.

I gasp for breath.

"What the hell was that about?" Mr. Clark glares at me.

I drag myself back to my seat. I look at my ripped collar. I just got this shirt.

"Someone tell me what the hell just happened," Mr. Clark yells.

The team jumps to fill in Mr. Clark on Damien's brother and his two friends. Mike lifts his bag and sits beside me. He pulls out two sandwiches and hands me one.

"Turkey."

"Thanks," I say.

"No worries."

"Yo?"

"Yo."

"We rocked 'em, didn't we?"

Mike takes a bite of his sandwich. "Yeah, we did." He grins.

Chapter 7 : Work

Write about a job you have held. Choose one incident, a series of incidents, or a period of time to demonstrate your experience of the job.

The Roti Shop

Selina Africaine

Mrs. Arthur bursts through the bead-curtained doorway. "Ifie, there is someone here to see you."

Mrs. Arthur and her husband own the Nostrand Roti Shop, a small West Indian restaurant in Brooklyn, New York. I work for the Arthurs—illegally, since I do not have immigration papers.

I look at Mrs. Arthur's flushed, walnut-coloured face and then at the three rotis baking on the stove. I hold another roti in my hand. I have everything going in a rhythm—the pans at the right temperature, the curries bubbling. I want to meet my quota: fifteen hundred rotis for the day and two huge pots of curry, one beef, the other chicken.

I have a few hours of work before knocking off for the day. I do not want to see anyone. The Arthurs have strict rules against employees bringing personal business into their restaurant. So far, I have complied with all the rules.

I want to tell whoever has come to see me to go away. I need this job. I have my mother, my daughter, my sister and her daughter and myself to take care of. I work illegally. Knowing how much I need this job, I never invite anyone to visit me.

I look apologetically at Mrs. Arthur. I glance at myself in the mirror on the wall near the doorway. White flour covers most of my skin and hair. I look down at my swollen, pained feet. I wear an old pair of Mr. Arthur's shoes. I pray for the hours to pass quickly. I want to get home and soak my feet in hot water and Epsom salts.

I cannot go out into the front of the restaurant looking the way I do.

"Girl, whey is this famous roti I hear you a mek?"

I know that baritone voice speaking in Guyanese creole.

"Rick!"

A handsome tall black man appears in the doorway. He grins mischievously.

"What are you doing here?"

Rick's grin does not seem to belong to the distinguished looking gentleman before me in a custom-made, three-piece wool suit and spit-polished, black winged-tipped shoes. He looks important and elegant, his well-groomed hair touched with grey at the temples. He looks like an African movie star. Rick is indeed an important man—he runs the Guyana Consulate in New York City.

My ex-boyfriend, Danny, introduced Rick to me, and when Danny and I broke up, Rick and I stayed friends. Rick treats me like a younger sister. He always checks on me to see how I am doing. My face beams when I see Rick come into the kitchen in the back of the Nostrand Roti Shop.

"What the hell?" Rick looks at me standing in the hot, steamy kitchen. The rotis begin to burn. "Get your coat. You are leaving here now!"

"She can't leave now, man." Mrs. Arthur seems just as angry. "Can't you see she is working?"

"Madam, this young woman is a very good friend of mine. She is not a slave and I will not have you treating her as one. I will not stand here and watch you exploit her this way. Do I make myself clear? If you do not let her leave right now, after you pay her whatever money you owe her for her service, I will call the immigration service and let you tell them why you are employing an illegal alien. All they will do to her is send her back to Canada."

"Alright, man," Mrs. Arthur says. "I don't want no trouble."

I have never seen Mrs. Arthur move so quick to get my wages. And for once, she has the correct amount. Mrs. Arthur short-changes her employees all the time.

I want to cry. I feel proud knowing that someone cares for me so much. But I also need my job. I stand dumbfounded as I watch the exchange between Rick and Mrs. Arthur.

As I get dressed into street clothes, I think about my family back home in Guyana. I wonder about how I am going to manage now that I don't have a job. I know that the Arthurs are ripping me off. I make fifteen hundred rotis a day. They sell each roti for two dollars. I work six days a week for one hundred dollars. They make seventeen thousand nine hundred dollars a week from the rotis I make. But I was grateful just to have a job. Compared to what some of my friends earn as illegal immigrants, without any special skills, I was doing better than most.

Rick guides me out to his limousine and holds open the door. I get in. Rick sits beside me.

"Ifie, don't worry girl," he says. "Everything will work out. I am sorry I had to do that, but I could not see you in that situation and let it go. You are my friend. If there is anything I can do for you, you know I will. I just want you to take care of yourself. Look at you, girl. You are so skinny. Look at your feet. I am sure your mother wouldn't want you to get two big feet. You have to learn to say, 'Fuck it!'"

Rick raises my worried face with his hand and looks into my eyes. "Say it. *Fuck it!* Come on, girl. Say it. *Fuck It!*"

I look at Rick and smile. I can't do anything about what just happened. I have to look for another job. I have to remember to never again tell Rick where I work. He keeps looking at me with his mischievous grin as he opens the door to let me out.

"Fuck it!" I say.

Rick grabs me into a bear hug. "That's my girl. You will be all right."

He grins again and returns to his limousine. I open the front door leading to my Brooklyn flat. The horn honks, the limousine pulls away, and Rick is gone. I stand at the door for a moment, then run up the stairs.

"Fuck it!" I scream in the quiet flat. "Fuck it!"

~~~

It took a while before I found another job. I never again told Rick where I worked. I knew he would never understand that any job I could find would be exploitative. I was, after all, an illegal immigrant, and I had family back home dependent on every penny I sent.

But sometimes I still say, "Fuck it!"

Flying Down to Rio

Penny Verbruggen

"B ut, can you write?" asks David, the young editor of *The Brock Press*.

"I think so."

"Well, you're an English major, aren't you? Terri said you're in his Chaucer class or something like that."

"CanLit, actually. He told me to ask you about some freelance work."

David sits behind a sticky cafeteria table. He reaches for his Bic pen, holds it in the air for a moment, then draws spirals on the edge of an empty Styrofoam coffee cup.

"What have you written?"

"Essays, mostly."

"Jesus. Jesus. Jesus." He pokes a hole through the white Styrofoam. A cellophane sandwich wrapper slips to the floor. "Terri's killing me. He's sending essay writers to me now. Shit."

David lifts his wire-rimmed glasses from a spiral-bound note-book, swings them around by an arm, and gives me an assignment.

"There's no pay 'til you prove you can write more than essays. Check out that Flying Down to Rio store on St. Paul Street. Bring back something around two hundred words. I need it in two days in the *Press* office. Second floor of the tower."

~~~

Flying Down to Rio sits between the Niagara Bicycle Shop and The Lancer restaurant in downtown St. Catharines. Battered mannequins pose freakishly in used clothing, worn feathered hats sit lopsided on hairless heads and cheap rhinestone jewellery dangles from three- and four-fingered hands. A hand-painted sign nailed above the sidewalk entrance reads "Flying Down to Rio."

I pull hard on the tarnished brass and glass doorknob and enter the dark store. Velvet dresses and blazers shiny from wear hang from a high ceiling. Clothes move rhythmically as two bamboo fans swirl overhead. Patched tweed blazers, faded corduroy overalls, crushed-velvet hip huggers and a gauzy mauve prom dress compete for space on a corner desk. A pewter cash register stands open.

"Hello? Mr. Carter? Hello?"

I poke around the merchandise. A black Indian cotton dress drapes over a shiny metal rack. When I lift the flared sleeve, a white linen peasant blouse with stained underarms slips to the hardwood floor. I place it on top the jumble of smelly garments that hang half on, half off their metal hangers. The store reeks of incense, pot, damp wood and body odour.

I hope Mr. S. Carter is in the office at the rear of the store. The door is closed, but he should be able to hear me—the plywood office walls don't reach the yellow, carved plaster ceiling. I turn sideways and push through the bundles and boxes of unpacked clothing that form tight aisles on my way to the gouged office door. Before I can knock, Mr. Carter rushes in the front door.

"Hey! Can I help you find something today?" He glances at the open cash register and then back at me. "Sorry. There's no fucking bathroom in this place. They let me piss at Diana Sweets. What'cha looking for today, eh?"

Mr. Carter steps around a pair of brown leather Jesus boots on the floor. He reaches over the cracked countertop and slams the cash drawer shut. A little orange Levi's tag shows against the black fabric of his skinny jeans.

"Mr. Carter, I'm Penny Verbruggen from *The Brock Press*. We have a three-thirty interview?"

"Oh, Peggy. That's right. I forgot about you. Call me Jack."

He rubs tobacco stained fingers across his chin stubble and pulls on his thin, greying ponytail. White curling hairs show through the embroidered edges of his green tunic top. He does not shake my extended hand.

"Jack?" I shrug and scratch out the *S* initial from my clipboard notes.

"Should we sit somewhere to do this?"

"No, no, no. You write away and I'll straighten up a bit. Follow me around a while and learn."

Jack steps away from the counter. "How old are you, Peggy? You don't look old enough to be in university."

"I'm in second year, sir. Jack, I mean. Listen, can I ask you some questions about your store? Like, how long you've been here? Where you get your stuff? What kinds of people shop here? What things sell the most?"

"Peggy, Peggy, Peggy. I thought you were here to interview *me*." Jack puts both hands on his chest. "People don't want to know about the store. Come on. They come for me, honey."

"I will be sure to include that in my notes, Jack." I scribble some shorthand notes about mannerisms, brown cigarette-stained fingers against a green shirt, and attitude. "Let's start with the store's name. You loved the movie?"

Jack rests an elbow on a wobbly rack. A metal hanger clangs to the floor. I bend, pick it up and hold it out to Jack.

"Just jam it where there's room, Peggy." Jack heads to the back of the store. "Tell you what, babe. Put down your notes and get dirty. You wanna learn about the store, you gotta work the store. See the people, take in the ambiance, maybe hang up a few items to get a feel for what's here. Dig?"

I spread my arms wide and look up at the fans. Whatever it takes, I think, and toss my clipboard. The closest rack is a mix of skirts, shirts, overalls, heavy coats, umbrellas, purses and a red plastic child's raincoat. I remove items with original price tags affixed to a sleeve or a collar.

"I go on buying trips, Peggy, to warehouses in Toronto. It's vintage. People like vintage. They don't like used. Off the record, between you and me, it's just people's used shit. Look at this stuff." Jack laughs and pulls a pack of cigarettes from under his shirt. "You smoke?" He offers me one.

"No, thank you."

"Nothing? Nada? Niet?"

"Pardon, sir?"

"You don't smoke anything?"

I pretend interest in the torn tie-dyed T-shirt in my hands, then shake my head. "No, nothing."

"You're not going to *mind* if I go backstage and light one, right?" Jack points to the makeshift office. I refold the T-shirt and shake my head again.

"Okay. Won't be long. A guy's gotta relax. How are you with windows?"

"Windows, sir?"

"Window dressing...the fine art of. Jodi did the last one. Not bad, just not as good as Angelee's. Bitches left me high and dry. When you're tired of folding, try dressing the dummies."

Jack laughs, goes behind the office door, and repeats "dressing the dummies" to his own ridiculous laughter. Cigarette smoke soon mixes with the scent of vintage.

"Oh, and if you want to train here for a couple of weeks, I can pay you to mind the shop part-time," Jack hollers from behind the cheap walls. "Prove yourself in the window and I'll consider paying you after, say, a couple of weeks. Show ya how to work cash, customers, orders. You know, the ropes."

"Thanks, Jack. I have to go now. There's enough research here for my article. Thank you for your time. Bye."

I hurry from Flying Down to Rio, step out onto St. Paul Street, and breathe in the cool April air. People walk past the storefront, check their reflections, and rush ahead. Behind me, Jack puts a ragged cardboard sign in the window with the word CLOSED scrawled in black marker. I look at the *S* scribbled out on my yellow notepad.

~~~

I climb the stairs to the second floor of the Brock Tower. A neat, professional sign glued to the door reads "BROCK PRESS." I carry my two-hundred-and-fifty-word article in a brown manila envelope to the editor's desk. Dave waves his fingers, indicating a pile of scratchpads, loose-leaf paper and a dictionary. Three empty Ruby Rouge wine bottles rest on their sides on a book bag behind his rolling chair.

"How many words?" he asks.

"Two hundred and fifty."

"Why so short? I have space to fill. Bruce fell through on his piece about Age of Majority cards. Fuck."

"You asked for two hundred words. I was afraid you'd be upset I'd gone over."

"Fuck!" Dave takes off his wire-rimmed glasses and throws them on his paperwork. He looks up. "Still here? Wha'd'ya want?"

"Well, I was wondering when I could pick up the payment for my article. Should I come back later today or tomorrow? It's just that I've never done this before."

"Ha!" Dave flings himself against the back of his chair. "Let's see if it's good. Let's see if it's enough. Let's see a track record before I start handing out money for nothing.

"Oh, say hi to Terri for me."

Attention

Shaan Gupta

I reach into the pocket of my chinos and pull out my iPhone. I click the home button and the screen comes to life. It reads 5:15 p.m. I have only been at work for an hour?

I lean against the glass showcase and stare out the door. An old man wearing a black toque walks along the sidewalk. His gaze focused on the ground, he bends down and picks up three cigarette butts. He pulls out a lighter, lights one of the butts, inhales the smoke, exhales, then walks back toward an alley beside The Curry Palace next door.

I've worked as a sales associate at Link It Up, at the corner of Hurontario and Dundas in Mississauga, for the past six years. My sister Riti is good friends with the owner of the store. Riti hooked me up with the job when I turned sixteen. I didn't even have to fill out a job application or go to an interview. I like to think I'm qualified for the job, though.

Katy Perry's "Hot N Cold" plays from speakers in the cracked ceiling tiles above me. I swear it's the millionth time I've heard the song today. Why do we get only one radio station? I look around the empty store. Dark blue walls. A white poster with a giant Samsung Galaxy smartphone. Another poster with the blue Bell Mobility logo. A small black sign with gold lettering says, "Warning, premises monitored by CCTV 24 hours." Metal bars cover the window. They remind me of a prison cell.

I hear a rustling from the back office and freeze.

Oh no, Amit's here. I need to pretend to be busy. I look around. Fingerprints stain the glass showcases…but I hate cleaning. Some phones in the display cases need their prices updated. Nah, too much work. Empty boxes on the counter behind me need to be thrown out. Perfect. Easy work.

As I pack the garbage can, I look up and see Amit walking towards me. Perfect timing.

"What are you doing?" asks Amit.

"I'm just cleaning up," I tell him. "I thought I should probably throw out all the junk before I start doing other work, right?"

I wait for an answer.

"That's completely unacceptable," he says in a stern voice.

My forehead feels moist. "I know. I need to work harder. I know my sales haven't been great this month, either. I promise I'm going to work on it."

I look at Amit for approval. He stares at me blankly.

"Vlad, can I put you on hold for a second? My employee is trying to say something to me." Amit raises his index finger and jabs his ear. "Shaan, what are you going on about?"

I look at his ear and see a black Motorola Bluetooth headset. My face turns red. "Oh, never mind. Nothing." Amit looks at me with a raised eyebrow and walks to the back office. I sigh.

The doorbell chimes. A man wearing a black do-rag swaggers in. Faded jeans hang from his knees. A black oversized sweatshirt covers everything in between.

"Yo, do you have any BlackBerries?" he asks in a deep voice.

"Definitely. What kind of BlackBerry were you looking for?" I reply with perhaps too much enthusiasm.

"What's the best one?"

"Well, that would have to be the BlackBerry Bold 9780. It has everything you would want in a smartphone: WiFi, a two mega-pixel camera, 3G, and of course you get BBM."

"Oh, sick. Lemme see that."

I unlock the first glass showcase and pull out a shiny BlackBerry. As I hand it to him, I see him staring at another smartphone beside it. "I see you're looking at the BlackBerry Curve 9300. That's a great phone. It doesn't have the same processing ability as the Bold, but the ergonomic design of the phone more than compensates for that."

"Sick. Lemme see that one, too."

I hand him the second phone. He holds a phone in each of his big, chalky hands. A few minutes go by and he continues to stare at the phones. I hope he picks the Bold. I'll make sick commission off that.

I turn my head and look out the glass door again. It's getting cloudy. I hope it doesn't rain.

BAM!

The glass showcase rattles. I swing my head to see what the commotion is about and the man no longer stands in front of me. Out of my side vision, I see a black blur, already halfway across the store. Two giant leaps and the doorbell chimes and the man disappears.

Fuck. I'm going to be in so much trouble.

I turn around and walk straight into the back office. Amit sits at his glass desk, staring at his computer screen. "Uh, A-A-Amit?" I stutter. My arms tremble.

He types on his keyboard.

"Amit!"

"Yes, Shaan?"

"Uh, a guy just ran away with a Bold and a Curve."

"What!" he yells. Where did he go?"

"Uh—"

Before I can reply, Amit jumps out of his black leather chair and bolts to the front of the store. He glares at the two empty stands in the row of neatly placed phones. His face turns red.

"I'm so sorry, Amit." I look at him and then look down at the ground. "I don't know what happened."

"What do you mean you don't know what happened?" Amit screams. He points at the empty phone stands. "How could you just hand him two phones worth a thousand dollars and let him leave with them?"

"I-I-I don't know, it all just happened so fast. One second I was helping him, then I looked away for a second, and then the next second he was gone."

"How many times have I told you to pay attention when helping out a customer?" Amit yells. "You're lucky you're Riti's little brother, otherwise this would be coming out of your paycheque!"

I shift my gaze to the glass door. The old man in the black toque still walks slowly along the sidewalk, looking at the ground. He stops, bends down and picks up another cigarette butt. He looks around and continues walking.

Jailbait

Bailey Green

The Girards sit at the same booth they sit in every Sunday.
Speaking in a cultured joual, they ask their waitress for more
raw sugar. They always drink three coffees each. They require four
packs per coffee. Debbie, her faded orange hair done up with black
chopsticks, trudges over to fetch their sugar packs, plods back, and
drops them on their table.

Beyond the vast concrete parking lot in front of the outlet mall,
cars speed east and west on Autoroute 40. The mid-morning sun
glares through Coco Java's floor-to-ceiling windows. Customers
enjoy a quiet brunch in the small restaurant on the outskirts of
Hudson, on the outskirts of the West Island, on the outskirts of
Montreal, Quebec.

Laughter from a table of middle-aged couples at the centre of the
dining room assaults my ears. I stride toward them with three mugs
of coffee in each hand. A bowl of mini milk and creamers teeters on
top.

I place the coffee cups from one hand on a vacant table beside
them and set down the other three cups of coffee on their table. As
I lift a cup from the empty table, a balding man in a business suit
shoves his chair back and into me. My knees buckle. Half a mug of
scalding coffee splashes over my hand.

"Ow!" I inhale sharply.

The table hushes. The bald man glowers at me. "You need to
watch where you're going sweetheart, that coffee just missed me."

My lips press into a thin line. "So sorry sir, my fault. I'll get you another coffee."

I rush back to the bar, pour a fresh cup and deliver it to the table. I dole out the remaining mugs. I apologize again.

The bell at the front door trills. Tony swaggers into the restaurant. A thin gold chain bounces against his collarbone. He catches my gaze and winks. My entire body itches as I hustle back to the counter where Debbie leans on the bar.

"Where's my toast order?" she asks.

"Coming, sorry!" I say.

Debbie hauls herself over to the swinging door that divides the kitchen from the restaurant. She pokes her head inside. "How much longer is my order gonna be?" she asks.

"Debbie, would you get off my ass?" Kostos, the head chef and owner, yells back.

"Cook faster and I will," she says and then fully inserts herself into the kitchen.

I toss four slices of bread onto the metal rack of the rotating industrial toaster. The singed red skin on my right hand throbs. I rush over to the sink and run cold water over my hand.

"Good morning, sexy." Tony struts up to me.

"Hey Tony, how are you?" I say.

He inhales through his teeth as his bulging eyes scan me up and down. "I'm great. Thanks for asking, jailbait. When do you turn seventeen again?"

"Never." I roll my eyes.

"Hey, what happened to your hand?" His voice softens.

"Some jerk shoved his chair into me. Acted like it was my fault, too," I say.

"Asshole. Aw, babe…" Tony pulls my hand from the water. His calloused hands encase my fingers as he examines the burn. The rough pad of his thumb brushes the vein on the back of my hand.

The toast tumbles out of the machine.

"'Scuse me, Tony." I pull my hand back.

"Not a problem," he says as I sidestep past him.

I butter the toast, cut it in half, and nestle it into a wicker basket. Debbie comes through the swinging kitchen door with two oval plates overflowing with eggs, bacon, fresh fruit and home fries. I slide the toast basket down to her. She catches it without slowing down. Her long nails slide through the gaps in the wicker.

Tony counts his float, the bills and coins for his shift, at the break table across from the bar. I sip a coffee with three creams and two sugars and remember that my *Of Mice and Men* essay is due tomorrow. I fidget with my black collared shirt and smooth my black tailored pants.

From the back of the kitchen comes an eruption of yelling in Greek. Kostos and his father, Spyros, argue constantly over how to run the restaurant; ownership has gone back and forth between them twice while I have worked here. I shake a bit of vinegar onto a clean linen cloth and begin polishing a tray of cutlery in case Kostos storms out.

"You look tired honey," Tony says.

"Not really, legs are a bit sore."

I immediately regret my choice of body part.

"How 'bout I massage them for ya?" Tony smiles a crooked smile.

"No thanks Tony, not that sore."

"How 'bout you come sit down?" He spreads his legs and pats his knee.

"Nope, I'm good."

"Come on, sit on Santa's lap and see what pops up," he says.

"Tony!" I sputter and avoid his eyes. "You're awful!"

He licks his front teeth.

Debbie lumbers towards us and leans against the counter. Her gold bangles clink against the faux marble bar. She swings her head to look at Tony. Her chunky hoop earrings pull down her earlobes.

"Good morning, Tony," she says.

"Good morning, beautiful," he says.

Debbie flicks her eyes to me. "He never stops, does he?"

"Not that I've seen," I say.

Tony scoffs.

I check the clock—eleven. I'm halfway through my shift.

"Could I order some food from you, Debbie?" I say.

"Sure." She pulls out her pad and pencil.

"Just the regular Eggs Benedict, please."

She passes my order to the kitchen as two families walk in. I grab a handful of menus and seat them in booths. Debbie gets the family with two adorable toddlers. Tony takes the family with the hot soccer mom.

"How're you all doing today?" Tony claps his hands and rubs them together.

I bus the table where the Girards messily devoured their brunch. I scrape kiwi rind and ketchup from their dirty dishes into the garbage can at the back of the bar.

Johnny pokes his head out of the small kitchen window. "Bailey, your food is ready."

"Aw, you made it yourself?" I beam at him. "Thanks so much."

"No problem. There's something special in it, too."

Johnny smiles. His straight white teeth glow against his dark skin. He folds his tall frame down to pass me my food through the window. I grasp the warm plate. My mouth floods with saliva at the smell of home fries. I place the plate on the break table and sit down. I slice into the first poached egg. The yolk oozes out like lava, coats the ham and English muffin, and melts into the buttery Hollandaise sauce. Perfect. I raise the fork to my mouth and my eyes widen. Two and a half layers of smoked salmon hide beneath the ham. I look back to the window.

Johnny nods shyly. He tucks a few stray curls of his enormous afro back into his hairnet.

"Johnny, what are you doing? Get your fucking head back in here and cook some shit," Kostos barks. "Let's go!"

"Yeah, boss." Johnny withdraws into the kitchen.

"I didn't promote you from dishie so you could chitchat all the fuckin—" The window slams shut.

Tony darts out from behind the bar. "So I have to make my own toast?" I nod. "It won't be as perfect as when you make it, baby."

"Shush your mouff, shtupid," I say.

Tony laughs, brews a fresh pot of coffee and tosses bread into the toaster. Johnny, apron stained with grease, emerges from the kitchen and places a rack of clean cutlery on the bar. Behind Tony's back, Johnny winks at me.

I devour another forkful of eggs benny.

Shit Tire: Fenelon Falls

Andrew Ihamaki

T en minutes to closing and Irwin's still riding my ass. Someone apparently didn't crush their own cardboard and somehow it's my fault. I hate working here.

"G'night, Andrew," Angie says as she leaves the store at the end of her shift. "Is everything okay?"

I stop and look at her. "Just fuckin' Irwin. What else is new?"

She nods. She knows. She's been there.

The once white floor tiles shine grey and yellow like a row of old smoker's teeth. Grease cakes every groove of the once pristine floor. Dust rounds off every corner. My feet kick through piles of dirt as I make my way to the cardboard crusher at the back of the store. I punch open the swinging doors, setting off an avalanche of flattened cardboard boxes.

Every box has "Tide" written on the side. They are clearly Shannon's from the housewares department. I don't open very many Tide boxes in the garden centre. Irwin is too stupid to make that connection. I let out a massive sigh and begin clearing a path to the crusher.

The radio hisses from my right hip pocket.

"Can I get a carry-out—" The radio cuts out. "Patio slabs."

I ignore the call. Tim can get it. Besides, Irwin already told me that crunching cardboard is my number one priority.

I force the cardboard into the machine's gaping mouth. I press the lever and watch it chew its meal.

"Is somebody coming for that carry-out?"

The cashier waits another minute and repeats the call. "Is some-one com—"

Irwin interrupts her over the radio. "Andrew, what're you doing? It's your job to do carry-outs. Answer her!"

All the employees can hear Irwin—and any customer who happens to be standing within ten feet of him. What an asshole.

"I'm doing cardboard like you said," I tell him over the radio. "Tim should be out there."

Irwin squawks back, "Your job is carry-outs. I don't care where Tim is. I'm telling you to do it."

I swallow every curse word I know.

I walk away from the crusher and make my way back through the store. I hope to see Irwin's little rat face on his giraffe neck of a body. I badly want to punch his bulgy bug eyes into the back of his head. But I don't see him. I step outside into the heat. Sweat instant-ly drips down my neck and back. The customer's truck sulks under the weight of five patio slabs and Tim on the flatbed. Janet shouldn't be lifting anything but she tries because no one else offered to help.

"How many more?" I ask.

"This makes six, so sixty-four," Tim says as he lays down a fifty-pound patio slab.

I look at my phone—5:55. The store closes at 6. I've been here since 7:30. I tell Janet she can leave, but she refuses. She knows that no one can go home until we're done. I work twice as hard so she doesn't have to help as much. Tim keeps up with me.

The edges of the slabs grind through the skin at the joints of my fingers. My hands cramp and my arms almost give out at the fortieth slab. Janet can't lift anymore but still tries to help.

Irwin's voice screams over our radios. "Andrew, why isn't the cardboard finished?"

I lay down another slab and answer him. "I'm helping Tim and Janet, like you told me to do."

I wait and don't hear an answer. It's 6:20 now. We quicken our pace. My hands are numb, my head pounds with exhaustion, and the feeling of battery acid pumping through my veins makes me nauseous. Irwin comes and yells at us.

"Janet, what're you doing?" he says.

"I'm helping these guys because nobody else would."

Irwin doesn't flinch. He doesn't even look at us. "They can do it themselves." Irwin turns to us as Janet leaves. "Hurry the hell up! Some of us want to go home tonight." He turns and follows Janet back inside.

The last slab slams onto the flatbed. Tim jumps from the truck onto the asphalt. He grabs his lunch bag and leaves. The driver tips his hat and pulls out. I bend over with my hands on my knees and catch my breath before I hurry inside and race up the stairs to the break room to gather my things. I hope Irwin doesn't see me. I'm exhausted. I have to be back in the morning at 7:30.

I bolt down the stairs, touching only three of the twelve steps. I stop at the punch-in computer. My fingers look like a blur as they key in my password. I hit Enter. The screen reads 6:55. I trip out the door to my car. I dig the keys out of my pocket as I approach the driver's side. I yank the door open. I plop myself into the seat and stick the key into the ignition.

Irwin pages me again.

"Andrew, the cardboard still isn't done! Where are you?" His voice echoes in the small interior of the car. I reach down and grab my radio. My fingers run along the seam of the plastic case and the antennae. They continue down and reach the volume dial.

"Andrew! Answer when I call you! Where are you?"

My index finger and thumb caress the dial.

"Andrew! And—"

Click.

I pull out of the parking lot.

Life Fifth-Period French

Vincent Gao

The sun blazes over the beach at Camp Kodiak in McKellar, Ontario—some tiny blip on the map near Parry Sound.

Kids run about and counsellors chase after them. A chubby brown kid collides with me and then asks me to train him for a marathon. I have no idea what he's talking about. He runs off. I retreat to the shade under the old pavilion and drape a towel over my shoulders.

I spot Jeff sitting on top of a picnic table cluttered with towels, water bottles and clothing. A scruffy grey beard sprouts from his chin. He probably hasn't shaved in a week and he looks like he hasn't slept in a week. A supply teacher in his late twenties, Jeff reminds me of a middle-aged mall-Santa.

"Hey, Jeff," I say. "How's it going?"

Jeff is in charge of a cabin of eighteen-year-olds with Down syndrome, Asperger syndrome and autism. Like me, it's his first summer working at Camp Kodiak.

"It goes." He offers me a lazy fist bump. "Where are your kids?"

"Fuck if I know, around probably."

We bump fists and I plop myself down beside Jeff. "I've set them free. If you love someone, set them free, right?"

A short, shrill whistle blasts from the dock. "Andy!" Sarah, in her lifeguard getup, screams at a tiny fifteen-year-old from Mexico, who probably splashed some kids or tried to climb on top of them or did something else obnoxious.

Andy looks at Sarah, splashes her from the water, and dives away before she can react.

Sarah and I, along with Blake, the head counsellor, live in a cabin with ten boys between thirteen and fifteen years old, all of them diagnosed with Attention Deficit Hyperactive Disorder. We are required to supervise them at all times, except during swim time when the lifeguards watch after them.

"Found Andy," I say. Andy is one of mine.

"All my kids are in the water today," Jeff says. He lets out a yawn. "Makes my life easier."

"What are you gonna do after camp?" I ask.

"I don't know, probably find a quiet place and jerk off." Jeff shrugs. "You?"

I need to find a quiet place to live after camp ends, before I head back for my third year at university. But I don't get a chance to respond. Nick, one of my fourteen year olds, sneaks up behind me and sprays me with his water bottle.

"Oh, hey boy number four," I say to Nick, paying no mind to his prank.

"Yeah, see," I turn back to Jeff. "I don't call them by their names, they get numbers instead. That there was boy number four."

Nick is still within earshot.

"Real proud of you, boy number four!" I announce, trying to sound fatherly. Nick wanders off.

"Vince, you are next level." Jeff chuckles.

Cold water splashes the back of my head. I turn around and find Nick dancing about with an empty bucket in his hand and a big-ass grin on his face. I glare at him with water dripping from my hair.

Nick laughs and runs off.

"Oh no, he didn't!" hollers John, a lanky thirteen-year-old from Ethiopia—another one of my boys, doing his best impression of a suburban black lady from Atlanta.

The black lady has spoken. I have to respond to Nick dumping water on me.

I rise from the picnic bench, slow and deliberate. "Boy, I'm gonna drop you like fifth-period French," I bellow at Nick. A small smirk sneaks its way onto my face.

People around us laugh.

"Hey, I used to supply for a French class," Jeff cuts in, feigning annoyance.

Someone tackles me from behind. It's Sam, the big fifteen-year-old from my cabin. That's the problem with teaching martial arts at camp—everyone wants to beat me up. I grab Sam's arm, flip him over my shoulder and dump him onto the beach sand. He lands with a soft thud. He's fine.

"He just done kung fu'd yo ass!" John declares.

I look back at Nick. He charges. My knee shoots up. I twist sideways and the blade of my foot flies for his throat. I don't really like sidekicks. People always see them coming. Nick sees it coming. He stops short. I pull back. I don't feel any contact. Nick goes down anyway.

Shit. Did I really just kick him? Did I really just kick a fourteen-year-old in the throat?

Nick rolls around on the ground, clutching his throat and laughing. "I got kicked by the kung fu master!" he announces.

"No you didn't." I grin and help him up. "You just want to say that…and I don't even know kung fu. I know everything except kung fu. Quit being racist."

Nick grins and winds up a big soccer kick aimed at my crotch. I cover up in time. His foot finds my knee.

"Ow!" he cries out.

A long whistle sounds from the lifeguards. Swim time ends. We round everyone up and head for our cabins.

"No, I'm gonna drop *your* mom like fifth-period French," John shouts at Arthur across the cabin from his bunk. They should be writing letters home.

"Oi, boy number three, boy number five, stop talking about your mothers," I call out from the other side of the cabin. "Did you guys write your letters yet?"

"I thought I was boy number three," Sam says behind me.

"Uh, whoever does something stupid gets to be boy number three," I respond.

Andy steps out of the shower wearing a towel and humps the air.

"Put your penis away, boy number three. Nobody is interested. Write your letter already," I say.

A short, blond-haired British man in his thirties steps into the cabin. "Hey guys."

Andy humps the air some more towards the man's direction.

"Hi, Andy."

"Hey, Blake," I say. "Welcome back."

Blake says hi and takes command. "Alright, who else needs a shower before dinner?" He scans the cabin. "Go take a shower Sam, you're filthy."

Sam goes to the shower, Andy goes back to his bunk and John and Arthur stop insulting each other's mothers.

I climb onto my several-sizes-too-small bunk bed and plug myself into my headphones.

"We Will Rise" by Arch Enemy floods my head with heavy riffs and guttural vocals.

They all look the same
In this sea of mediocrity
I can be anything
Anything I want to be

I am the enemy
I am the anti—

Someone taps me on my leg. I slip off my headphones.

"Vince?" Nick looks up at me.

"Yes, boy number four?" I look down at him.

"If my parents got divorced and somehow you became my step-dad..." Nick's voice trails off.

Holy shit, this is heavy. I study Nick's expression, not sure how to react. As far as I know, his parents are happily married.

"...you'll be the only one I'll call 'Daddy,'" Nick finishes, his face impassive, not betraying a hint of expression.

If my parents got divorced and somehow you became my stepdad, you'll be the only one I'll call Daddy. Nick's words echo in my head.

Is this a prank? It has to be a prank. I scan the cabin for clues. No one in the cabin seems to have heard Nick, not even Blake, whose eyes and ears never miss a thing. I stare at Nick some more. Part of me wonders if he's serious. Part of me wants to flash him a big grin and ask him if his mom is hot. Part of me just wants to get back to Arch Enemy.

Nick looks at me, nods his head, and bursts into laughter.

I smile and slip my headphones back on.

Cash Three

Sami Karaman

"My boss hates me," I explain to Mom. "She always makes me the main cashier. I've been there for three years. I've got seniority over all these high school kids, but she lets them do whatever they want. Me, I'm trapped on Cash Three."

I work at Shoppers Drug Mart. It's Sunday and I'm scheduled to work two to nine. I wake up at noon and lie in my bed, depressed and in denial. The shift is a huge chunk of my day. Seven hours of sunlight and road hockey time down the drain so that I can stand at a cash register all day and ask customers if they have an Optimum card.

I tell myself today will be different. I will be the fourth worker in for the shift, so I will be assigned to cash register one or five, both located at the far ends of the store, out of sight—beautiful.

I get out of bed and prepare myself for the torture. I have a hurried breakfast and tell Mom that I'm going to quit soon. She yells at me and asks how I will earn money.

"I don't know." I shrug. "Allowance?"

Mom merely smirks.

I drive along Winston Churchill Boulevard in the blazing heat and make a left into Meadowvale Town Centre. It's 1:55. My supervisor demands that I arrive at work ten minutes early to count my till.

A sign hangs in the store entranceway: "Live, Love, Laugh, Shoppers Drug Mart." I really hope people don't fall for that ploy.

Shoppers couldn't care less if you lived, loved or laughed, so long as you purchase their overpriced goods.

I clock in at 1:58. I knock on the door that leads to my worst nightmare: Rita. Her fiery red hair shakes as she swings open the door. She gives me a fake smile, showing ugly teeth stained yellow from years of smoking. "You're late. Come in and count your till."

I count the money and contemplate how her deep voice sounds like a man's. If she ever fires me, I'll be sure to mention this to her on my way out the door.

"Hey, move over to five," Rita speaks into the phone. "Thanks. Bye."

I give her the filthiest, most hateful look I can muster.

"You'll be on Cash Three. Rebecca is moving for you."

"Okay," I mumble. I feel my face steadily redden as I walk away.

The line-up at Cash Three looks long. A whole bunch of people check their watches and sigh. I slip my till into the register and begin my robotic actions.

"Hello. Do you have an Optimum card?" I say to the first customer, an old lady with wrinkly skin. She slams three bags of milk onto the counter and inserts her debit card into the reader before I even have the chance to scan her products. "I haven't scanned your things yet," I say in a flat tone.

"Hmm?" she croaks.

"Please take your card out."

I scan the sticky, smelly, slimy bags of milk. "Do you need any bags?" I ask. "They're five cents."

"Eh? No."

She inserts her card again.

"Please take it out and wait for the message to pop up."

She must be deaf.

I take out her card and insert it at the correct moment. I look up and gasp at the huge line behind the old lady. Then I see Rebecca, who finished putting her till in register five, walk away.

"Hey, Rebecca," I yell. "Um, maybe you should open."

"Call Kelsey," she tells me.

I bend down and find the phone to make a page. I clear my throat. "Kelsey to ca—"

"Where are my bags?" the old lady interrupts me.

I hang up the phone, embarrassed at my failure to finish the page, and hope that Kelsey got the hint.

"I asked you if you wanted any," I say. "They're five cents."

"No." She shakes her head. Her wrinkly chin jiggles. "No, you didn't ask. Gimme three bags!"

I bag her milk and push it to the side of the counter to indicate that I want her to get out of the way. Kelsey, meanwhile, appears next to me on cash two. "Where's Rebecca?" she asks.

"No clue," I mumble.

"Well, next time call her."

Kelsey and I kill off the line, then she leaves. I look at the clock— it's only 2:10. Six more hours and fifty more minutes of standing in the same spot and dealing with the same shit.

I make petty conversation with some hot girls buying tampons and makeup. This lessens my anger. I figure I should make the best out of my day.

A large lady with a cart full of stuff approaches my counter. She is very friendly and all, but I can feel something's up.

"I have coupons," she says.

"Okay," I say. "For what?"

"Everything."

She pulls a binder out of her cart and opens it to reveal row upon row of coupons. She takes them out, one by one. I check the expiry date on each coupon. A line forms behind her. I tell myself to calm down as I process the tenth coupon. At the fifteenth, I feel like crying. The last coupon, the twenty-third one, has expired.

"Sorry, ma'am," I say. "I can't accept this one. It's expired."

"Let me see." She snatches it from me. "Ah, okay. Never mind."

She puts her hand out.

"Um, what?" I ask.

"I'd like all the coupons back. I'll come by some other time."

I hand the coupons back and she walks away leaving her twenty-three items scattered over my counter.

"Is there someone else you could call?" asks a lady from the back of the line.

I bend down to page Kelsey again, but before I can pick up the phone, I hear a voice behind me say, "Excuse me?" I look up and see a young girl with a five-dollar bill in her hand. "Could I get bus money?"

"When my till opens, yes." I turn back to the phone.

"No, I need it now," she says. "My bus leaves in five minutes. I'd like five loonies."

"I'm sorry. I can only open my till during a cash transaction." I clear my throat and finally speak into the phone. "Kelsey to cash."

As Kelsey and I work through the line, every customer pays with debit or credit cards. The young girl folds her arms and grits her teeth. "I want to speak to your manager!" she says. She looks close to crying.

"Um," I begin. "Sorry, she's unavail—"

"Don't be an ass," Kelsey says. She has an evil look in her eyes. She smells blood. What is it with women hating me? Does Mom even love me?

"She wants to talk to Rita. So, let her."

"Excuse me."

I turn and recognize the coupon lady. "Um, yes," I say.

"You didn't give me back all the coupons," she says.

Meanwhile, Kelsey has called Rita, who waddles up and gives the little girl a hug.

"Actually, I did," I tell the coupon woman, trying to sound polite in front of Rita. I look towards Rita and get caught up in the exchange between her and the young girl who recounts her story through sniffles and sobs. The hot girls with their tampons and makeup return my weak smile with looks of disgust as they learn about my ruthless, non-gentleman-like behaviour.

"I can't find my coupons for the Tide," the coupon lady persists. "Can you check?"

"I don't have your coupons!" I scream. It isn't a soft scream, either. I didn't mean to yell. I pause and look apologetic. Rita glares at me while she hands the little girl five loonies and doesn't even take her five-dollar bill.

"You can stay until ten today for what you did to that little girl," Rita says loud enough for everyone to hear.

I look at the people in line. They nod in support of Rita's decision. I half expect them to throw stones at me and leave me bleeding in some ditch.

"And ma'am, I have a ten-dollar gas card for you," Rita says to the coupon lady. "Compensation for the," she pauses and glares at me with a disturbing smile, "poor service."

Pot 'O Gold

Sara Middleton

E d raises his empty beer bottle. I meet his tired eyes and nod in acknowledgement. I walk back to the bar, open the beer fridge and grab him another Canadian.

"Thanks, sweetie."

Ed lives in one of the rooms above the restaurant. He is here every day and still doesn't remember my name. His unpaid tab runs to about seven hundred dollars worth of beer and the occasional pie. I don't know why my boss, Steve, lets him run his tab so high. Ed's monthly disability cheque barely covers his rent.

It's been a slow day at the Pot 'O Gold. Outside, the sun has finally set as my eleven-hour shift comes to a close. Just Steve and I work tonight. He cooks, I wait on the tables.

I make a cursory round of the restaurant and check on the two occupied tables. I politely chat with the customers, ask if their food is fine, and fill their water glasses. I look around at the newly-renovated space. Working here the past six months has been hectic. We had to close different sections at a time for painting, tiling and sanding. The restaurant now looks new. The marble countertop at the bar adds a little class.

I hear a ring and see Jerry walk in the door, whipping back his long hair. He's already tripping over his feet and a dumb smile is plastered on his face. His lips suck in oddly because of his missing front teeth. When he sees me, Jerry's smile widens. "Hey, sweetie," he slurs.

He sits across from me at the bar. "Beer and a shot, honey! What's your name again? Rachel?"

"I've told you three times this week, Jerry," I reply and grab a Budweiser and a shot of Southern Comfort.

"Ha-ha, well shit," he muses and slaps his knee. "Is it Rachel?"

"Sure," I lie.

I set Jerry's drinks in front of him. He grabs my hand and looks earnestly into my eyes. "Hon, do you realize how beautiful you are? Do you have a boyfriend, sweetie?"

I look away and see Steve's dark eyes dart away from mine. His large frame leans casually against the counter about ten feet away in the open kitchen. Steve suddenly appears interested in the traffic outside.

"No." I pull my hand back from Jerry.

"Aw, well, that's too bad, a pretty girl like you. Don't you think so, Steve-O?" Steve eyes flit to mine, then look quickly away. He gives Jerry a half smile.

"Three shots!" Jerry yells. "One for me, one for Steve, and one for you, pretty lady."

I look to Steve for consent and pour three shots of Southern Comfort. Steve saunters over. We all say "cheers" and down our shots. Jerry tells Steve, "Hey, Steve, don't you think it's a shame that my sweetie here has no boyfriend? She's so pretty. Someone is going to want to snatch her up for a wife soon, eh?"

"Uh, yeah," he mumbles. Steve, not usually lost for words, stays silent. He squeezes by me and makes himself a drink of vodka and 7Up. He gulps it and then sits beside Jerry. Steve turns the conversation elsewhere until Jerry asks, "Hey, Steve, how's the wife?" I quickly look over at Steve but he doesn't meet my eyes.

"What wife, Jerry?" Steve asks in an offhand way. "I'm single."

"Oh, you know, the pretty girl with the long dark hair and huge knockers that comes in here. She told me she was your wife."

Jerry must be talking about Olivia.

"Nah, she's not my wife. I'm living the single life." Steve plays with a blue elastic band around his wrist. He doesn't look at me. I pretend to busy myself, unnecessarily filling water jugs. I make the excuse of needing to check on the customers and walk away. I don't want to listen anymore.

My tables are fine so I head downstairs to restock. The restaurant is in an old building and the basement ceiling is so low I can barely stand upright. The heat is stifling and the lighting dim. The basement runs the length of the restaurant and is stocked floor-to-ceiling with supplies. I head to the left where Steve has a small office. He keeps the red wine and vodka there and we're running low on both.

I turn on the light. I remember the times Steve and I sneaked kisses down here during shifts.

Steve and I dated in secret for a couple of months. We both thought it would be better not to mention that the owner was dating the waitress. We were going to wait until I returned to school to let the secret out. But our relationship ended four weeks ago when Steve found out his ex-girlfriend, Olivia, was pregnant with his child.

The same night Steve found out about Olivia's pregnancy, we finally had sex for the first and only time. Every time I look at him now I picture us rolling around in my bed together. It's hard to meet his eyes without cringing. We try to put on an act of normalcy. It seems to work. No one has said anything.

When I head back upstairs with the bottles in my arms, I see Steve, Jerry and Ed down another shot. My two tables are ready to leave. I tally up their bill and cash them out. I pocket eight dollars in tips. There's only the four of us left. Jerry buys me and the others a couple more shots while he rants about his ex-wife being a "spiteful bitch."

Steve decides to close up a bit early. I go about my closing duties. Because of the alcohol in my veins, it takes me a bit longer than normal to sweep and finish restocking.

Steve, Jerry and Ed continue to drink.

Half an hour later, Steve kicks them out of the restaurant with the excuse that he has to head to bed. The circles under his eyes have grown steadily darker. Jerry and Ed drunkenly stumble from the restaurant. Steve locks the door behind them. I turn off the back lights. Steve grabs the ashtray from behind the counter and we both light up a cigarette at the bar. We're both a bit tipsy.

We make some halting conversation. Steve makes us a drink, mostly vodka with a little 7Up, and we sit at the bar together, sip our drinks, and smoke.

I stare at the vases full of flowers that sit atop the bar, given to me and the other waitresses by male customers. Many of the flowers have been given by Jerry.

After a minute of awkward silence, I turn to Steve and boldly ask, "So, how are things with you and Olivia?"

"Ah, things look good," he replies, seemingly absorbed in the straw he swirls in his drink.

"What does that mean?"

He looks at me sideways and quietly responds, "I think she's going to have an abortion."

"Oh."

I'm a little stunned.

Steve watches my face for a reaction. I keep it blank and wait for him to go on.

"Olivia decided she wants to go back to Africa to work for the U.N. I don't want to be with her, but I'm not going to be a dick while she's carrying my child." Steve lets out a sigh and takes a drag of his smoke. "I'm going to play it cool. I think she's going to decide to have an abortion on her own. She never wanted children."

We sit in silence again. I finish my drink, put out my smoke and stand up. "I should probably head out. I do have to be here again at ten a.m."

Steve nods, stretches and stands up.

"I have to open tomorrow at five," he laughs.

Steve gives me a shy smile and opens his arms for a hug. I hug him and he buries his face in my hair. I've missed the feel of his big arms around me, but I pull away. When I do, Steve leans down for a kiss. I turn my head slightly and instead reach up and kiss him on the cheek. He smiles at me, as if that was his intention. I don't meet his eyes as I softly say, "See you tomorrow, Steve."

"Have a good night, sweetie!" He turns around, grabs a cloth and wipes down the counter.

I stumble over my feet as I walk out the front doors of the Pot 'O Gold onto Lake Shore Boulevard. The sound of city traffic slams my ears. Across the street, Jackie gives me a sombre wave. She's already working the corner. I wave back and sit down on a bench.

I watch Steve in the glow of the window while I wait for a street-car.

Chapter 8: The Interview

Interview someone about something that interests you, and produce a piece using material collected in the interview.

Lessons in Interviewing

Mike Novak

F rank sits in a wooden chair, his fingers interlocked. The grand-father clock in the hallway clicks. Chimes echo throughout the house.

"You want a beer?" he asks.

"Yeah, sure."

"Go to the basement and get two from the fridge."

I leave my list of questions and tape recorder on the kitchen table, head down to the end of the hallway and turn left to the basement as I have done so many times before.

"Are these the questions you're going to ask me?" Frank shouts.

"Yeah," I reply from halfway down the stairs.

"Mind if I read them?"

"Ah, sure," I say. "They are just kind of something to guide the conversation, in case I don't know what to ask. I figured we would just chat."

The fridge in the basement houses six-packs of Steam Whistle and Corona. It used to overflow with beer.

~~~

I first met Frank twenty-one years ago, after my family moved to Oakville. Frank, his wife, Anna, and his mother-in-law, Rina, lived next door. I was fifteen, Frank twenty-six.

Our neighbourhood consisted of business executives, a judge, a lawyer and a few doctors. Frank had long hair and a beard. He wore a white T-shirt under a dirty jean jacket and blue jeans ripped at the knees. He smoked cigarettes in the front yard and drank beer in his garage. He drove a rusty, old Honda Accord. We often didn't see him come home for days at a time.

Frank made my traditional Eastern European parents nervous until he formally introduced himself as Francois Gougeon, a sergeant in the RCMP drug unit. After that, our families regularly congregated in Frank and Anna's garage on summer nights. We drank beer and wine, ate Rina's homemade Italian sweets and listened to Frank tell stories about takedowns and bad guys. Frank took pride in driving fast, in taking risks and in arresting guys in unconventional ways. He enjoyed telling us about it.

Frank and I competed for who had longer hair. We prepped his driveway for paving and drank beer. We built a fence with a gate between our yards and drank beer. We laid matching interlock around both houses and drank beer. Frank taught me how to swear in Québécois French.

Frank still lives in the same house with Anna and his mother-in-law, but now he has two kids, a dog and a Subaru station wagon.

~~~

I grab two green bottles of Steam Whistle and head back upstairs.

"You're gonna ask me about my childhood?" Frank looks at me.

"I don't have to. We don't have to talk about it, if you don't want to."

Frank points to the tape recorder on the table. "You're going to record the conversation?"

"Yeah. I figured it would be more natural if I didn't have to scribble notes in the middle of our conversation."

Frank taps his finger on the paper that lies between us. "Okay, let's get started then."

"Alright." I press the record button. I wait.

Frank crosses his arms, rests his elbows on the kitchen table, and leans in. Then he leans back, takes a sip of his beer and taps the first question on the sheet of paper. "Okay, let's do the questions."

"So you grew up in Montreal, right?"

"Yes, in a middle-class neighbourhood. Kind of upper class and middle class."

"Kind of like Oakville?" I ask in my best reporter voice.

"Can you pause the recording?"

"Sure." I pause the recorder. "What's up?"

"Okay. In my job I do a lot of interviews. I teach people how to interview. You should ask me an open question, like, 'Where did you grow up?' And I'd say, 'In Montreal.' But if you ask in a way that is telling me the answer, you won't get an answer out of me. Okay? Let's try it again."

I press record.

"So, where did you grow up?"

"I grew up in a middle-class neighborhood. Kind of upper class and middle class together."

"Kind of like Oakville?"

"Yes." He nods. "Something like that."

We methodically go through my list of questions about childhood friends and school. Frank answers each point at length. Professional and poised, he occasionally pauses and scratches his goatee. I try to steer the interview into more casual conversation and ask questions outside my list, but each attempt is thwarted and Frank points to the next question on the list.

I finally crunch through to questions about Frank's job. I have heard some great stories about biker wars, drug smuggling, stakeouts and middle-of-the-night raids and about being the prime minister's bodyguard and driver.

"What was the most exciting takedown in your career as an RCMP officer?" I tap my pen on top of my hand.

"I don't like to tell stories about that."

"Okay." I pause and my eyes blink a few times. What? All those summer nights when we sat in the backyard with friends were usually abuzz with action stories about arrests. Now he chooses not to talk about it? Frank has a serious face on, his professional face—one that I haven't seen before. He is an RCMP officer now, being asked about his work.

We move on through the interview. The look in his eyes and his posture change when I ask him about the most significant event of his life.

"When my kids were born," he replies. "I just want them to have the best and to grow up safe."

I gather the two pages of questions into a bundle.

"Well, that's it." I stop the recorder. "We're done!"

Frank sits back in his chair. He lowers his shoulders and his voice relaxes. "Man, I've interviewed a lot of people." He takes a sip from the beer he holds. "We have to do it all the time. You have to know how to do it and with each person it's different. It's all in how you ask the question. Sometimes the best question is silence."

I nod, pick up my beer and lean back in my chair. The two of us sit quietly. I stare at the questions, the pen, the recorder on the table.

"Sometimes you ask a guy a question and he doesn't give you the answer right away. So you just sit there in silence after he finishes talking. They usually get awkward and then they start talking. That's when the goods come out. You just have to wait for it. You also have to know how to ask the question.

Some people have it, some don't. You have to get under their skin."

"It's part psychology," I say.

Frank nods, takes another sip, and continues. "Some people are just dying to get it off their chest. They've been doing bad stuff for so long, that they need to get it out and tell someone. Even if you're a cop and they know you're on the other side, they will tell you. And some people, you have to know how to get them to open up.

"I arrested this huge Italian guy. Muscles like this." Frank's palm hovers three inches above his bicep. "Big guy! I know that he's Italian. So, chances are he is close to his mom.

"Before I go into the room, I ask if anyone checked his wallet when they booked him. We usually take their wallets and then give them back. 'Does he have any kids?' I ask.

"'Yeah, I saw two pictures in his wallet,' the attendant says.

"I go in and sit down across from him. He sits there all puffed up, with his shoulders up and arms to the sides, trying to make himself as big as possible."

Frank leans in towards me. His face turns stern. "'How you doin?' I ask him.

"'What?' the guy says.

"'I said how you doin' today?'

"'How the fuck do you think I'm doin'?' he says. 'What the fuck is that supposed to mean? What kind of question is that?'

"'It's a normal question,' I tell him. 'I just want to know how you are, that's all.'

"'How the fuck do you think I am? I'm sitting here under arrest,' he says back to me. 'Things are shit.'

"I say to him, 'Are you close to your mom?'

"'Leave my mom out of this,' he yells back.

"'No, man. Are you close to your mom? Do you love your mom?' I know he's Italian, so chances are that he is really close to his mom. Most Italians are.

"'Yeah,' he says. 'I am close to her.'"

Frank leans in even closer and stares me straight in the eye. "'Well, you're a loser,' I say to him. 'You wanna know why? Because she's gonna be really disappointed in you and what you've done. You've let her down. Show me your wallet.'

"'Fuck that!' he says.

"'I said, show me your wallet. Or I can get a bunch of friends in here to help me get it from you.'

"'Fine,' he says and gives me his wallet.

"I open it and show him the pictures of his kids. 'Man, they're young,' I say. 'But you won't be there for their birthdays or hockey games or school plays. You're gonna be in jail, buddy—and for a long time. How do you think they will feel when they find out that their daddy is going to jail? You're a loser. You let them down, too. Yup, you fucked up big time.'

"At this point, he is just staring at me, not saying a word. So I tell him, 'Listen, I run the show here. I will be your executor. You start talking and we can work something out. You can be there for those special moments. You screwed up, but here is your chance to make it better. I'm gonna go get a drink. You can do some thinking. And when I get back, you better have a decision. Don't fuck things up even more. Do it for your kids, man.'

"So I walk out of the room. I see through the glass that this guy is crying. At this point I know I got him and I go get a drink of water. When I get back, he's ready to talk. He tells me everything. He would do anything to stay out of jail. He became an informant and he helped take down a lot of people.

"It doesn't always work, but most of the time you can get the info. You just have to know how to ask for it."

We sit back. The grandfather clock chimes again and we finish what's left of our beer and then head outside. Frank lights up a slim and we part ways.

The First Stop

Rachel James

S amantha stands across from me in the hallway. We wait for a shelter worker to unlock the office door.

"Today has been a good day," Samantha says. "I got second stage housing."

Samantha has an unequivocal smile that I instantly mirror back. At twenty, her long legs and long arms move with an awkward, innocent grace. She has straight blonde hair and almost imperceptible freckles.

"That's amazing!" I say. "What exactly does that mean?"

"Well, I get my own room and the door can lock. It's one step closer to housing."

Samantha pokes the tip of her slipper into the plush red carpet. The walls are covered in red and gold patterned wallpaper. The second-floor hallway of the shelter looks like a motel, but with brighter lights. The shelter worker finally arrives with a six-inch ring of clanking keys.

"Sorry it took so long," she huffs and opens the door.

Two desks, scattered with papers and Post-it notes, stand on either side of the room. I shut the door and turn one of the office chairs to face Samantha. Her fingers play with the cotton folds of her black sweatpants. She wears a loose-knit yellow sweater and a white and orange striped T-shirt. I remember, despite the public atmosphere, that we are in her home. She relaxes back in her chair, her long legs leaning to one side.

I met Samantha a few weeks earlier. Four graduate students and I had set up a meeting at the YWCA to see if there was interest in publishing an arts magazine. Only Samantha showed up the first week.

"Is this the meeting for the arts magazine?" she asked with hesitation, cradling a notebook and pen. Later, I asked if she was interested in being interviewed and Samantha said, "Yes."

⁓

I turn on the tape recorder.

"Let's start with your name, age, and where we are."

"My name is Samantha O'Conner. I'm twenty years old. Right now I'm living in a shelter with about forty other women. I've been here since December 3, 2009. I'm living here and going to school and it's basically because..." Samantha stiffens for a moment. "Okay, how am I going to say this?"

There is a brief, but intense, silence.

"I was brought up in a family with two mentally ill, abusive parents who were addicts. They met in AA and they beat me and my little brothers. My mom used to beat me with a two-by-four. She called it the Board of Education. She locked me in my room every single night.

"My mom is an evangelical Christian. She is prone to addiction. She went from drugs to alcohol to religion. Now she thinks that everything she does is justified by God. That's why she can beat me with a two-by-four and get away with it. Because it says in the Bible, 'Spare the rod, spoil the child.'"

Samantha speaks quickly but with ease. She says the words as if she has said them many times before. Her young voice carries conviction.

"I grew up in Winchester, Ontario, about half an hour outside of Ottawa. I lived with my mom, my dad and my two brothers. We stayed active. We loved school and we hated going home."

"Did you talk about your home life with your classmates?" I ask.

"No! I didn't even realize I was abused until I was eighteen years old. It was an epiphany. I remember the exact day—where I was, the smells, what I was wearing. I was in a motel room.

"My boyfriend lived in Niagara Falls and he was coming to visit me for my birthday. I got into a huge fight with my parents. By the time he drove the eight hours to my house, I already had my bags packed and thrown out the window. We decided to stay in a motel that night. I remember bawling my eyes out and thinking, Look where we are? We are in a motel room in Gananoque! Then I realized, Oh my god, I've been abused.

"I knew my mom hit me and did crazy stuff. We never got along. But I never took in the fact that I was abused. That means something. I realized that all the things I was doing in my life were because of the abuse. I was on this fast track—partying and not caring about my future. My brain was just shook.

"All the moments in my life flashed before my eyes. 'Look where we are?' I said. 'We are in a motel room in Gananoque!' I said the exact same lines, but this time I was laughing. My perspective totally changed. I thought—I am safe. I am safer than I was before."

"So what did you do after that?"

"I moved in with my boyfriend. I worked on a fruit farm. It was the best summer ever. I got accepted to the University of Guelph-Humber Media Studies program and we moved to Toronto. I made it through two years of university just fine. We had a cat and all that stuff. When we broke up, he kicked me out of the house.

"I had nowhere to go, so I called my parents. I told them that I needed to come home and work. I took a semester off. I decided to try to fix things with my parents. I thought I couldn't make it without them. I was working three jobs but I didn't even last a month at home. My mom had one of her bipolar attacks. She's a rapid cycler. She said, 'You're twenty, get off my property!' She called the cops.

"It's the most frustrating thing in the whole world, when you're screaming on the inside but you have to be calm and collected to police officers. If I freaked out, they would have taken my mom's side. So, I had to think about it and be smart about it."

I try to visualize the scene in my mind. It's hard to imagine the radiant, confident girl sitting in front of me in such a situation.

"What was your mother saying about you?" I ask.

"That I'm a dope head! That I'm a crazy, abusive girl! Everything that she is, she switched and said it was me. I ended up in an Ottawa shelter called Naomi's Family Resource Centre. I stayed there from Thanksgiving until the first week of December.

"I needed to go back to school. The shelter workers in Ottawa were like, 'How are we going to get you to Toronto?' They called around to all the different shelters in Toronto and they found a bed here. They called December 2 and said, 'Alright, we have a bed for you.' I had twenty-four hours to get from Ottawa to Toronto. On December 3, I made it all the way here, all by myself."

"What has it been like being twenty and entering the shelter system?"

"A lot of the women here are in their forties and fifties. I have more time to get my life together and I know I will. I have to learn all these lessons quick and hard."

"What has given you such a positive outlook?"

"Well, I had taken the negative self-pity route. I used to cry myself to sleep every night and think, Why me? I fell into a clinical depression. Then I realized that my life was more negatively affected the more negatively I thought. It wasn't until I totally flipped things and started living positively that I felt, All right, bring it on. Give it to me."

Samantha laughs.

"You told me about your mom. What was your father like?"

"My dad is a very weak man. I lived with him until I was eighteen, yet I didn't really know him. He's so secretive. He was married before he met my mom. That's when he was an alcoholic and his ex-wife used to beat him. He's got claw marks on his arms.

"He never did anything when my mom beat me. She was the one who hit us. He never laid a hand on us, but he never did anything to stop it. I don't have anything to say to him."

"Now, in your life, who is the most important person?" I ask.

"I am the most important person in my life. I don't have parents who are going to help me. I don't have people telling me I'm doing a good job. So, the only person I do this for, is myself. Otherwise, I'll be left behind in the dirt. I won't be able to do all the things I want to do."

Samantha is undeniably ambitious. I wonder how she manages living in the shelter as a full-time student. "What are the challenges of navigating the shelter system?"

"Half the workers are here because they want to help. To the other half, it's just a job. They got into this business because they like the control. They love being able to tell us what to do. Instead of talking to my workers, I talk to the women I live with. There are some mature women here who have been through a hell of a lot in their lives. I'm pretty sure I can learn more from them than from someone who went to school and read a bunch of textbooks."

"Have you made any close friends here?"

"Definitely."

"Will you stay in contact?"

"Definitely. I've never really had women role models in my life. I finally know some women who I look up to. Even though they're living here and they're going through some tough times, they keep strong. They are the strongest women who I've ever met in my whole life."

"Do you speak about your experiences of homelessness at school?"

"I'm in this journalism class called Presentation and Persuasion. It's a public speaking course. Every week, we give a speech. The first week I stood in front of my whole class and said, 'There are over a hundred and fifty thousand homeless people in Canada'—Samantha pauses for effect—'and I am one of them.'

"Their mouths literally dropped! I shared my story and broke the stereotype. I told people that homeless youth are not rebellious, not lazy, not bums. It just so happens that I was born into a situation beyond my control and I have to deal with it the best I can. I definitely made a difference in my class. I took my moment." Samantha laughs. "A lot of people mentioned 'bums' and 'homeless people' in their speeches. 'When you see a bum on the street...' I went up there and said, 'I'm homeless.'

"I'm kind of leading a double life. I'm doing really well in my program. I'm always participating in class, doing my work, and I have a social life. So no one would ever expect me to be homeless and living in a shelter. It changed their perspective and everyone has mad respect for me. They respect me for not being respected." Samantha laughs again. "Does that make any sense?"

I glance down at the list of questions I had typed earlier in the day. Samantha needs little prompting—it's the first time I've looked at the page. One question pops out at me.

"Have you had any experiences in your life that you consider sacred?"

"Definitely," Samantha says. "I've been through so much, but I've done so much. My opa is a horse whisperer and I was brought up on a horse farm. My first memories are of horses giving birth. At the age of twelve, I'd get on wild horses and teach them how to ride—break them, that's what they call it. I would just jump on the back of a bucking wild horse."

Samantha sits straighter and pauses.

"My life is slowly unfolding before my eyes. That's why every night I go to bed and visualize my dreams. I visualize being a successful journalist. I visualize myself travelling all over the world. I visualize all the things I want because I know they are going to happen."

Her conviction inspires and troubles me.

"The first twenty years have been lessons, the next twenty will be blessings." Samantha mouths the words as if casting a spell.

I recall my own life. No adequate summation for any person seems possible. But Samantha is convincing and my uncertainty feels like betrayal. I look down at the crumpled page of questions.

"Do you have advice to give to other girls or young women who might experience homelessness in the future?"

"Take as much as you can and don't look down on yourself. Don't look at yourself as homeless. You are on your way to being free from all that baggage from the past. Know that there are people out there willing to help. You are not alone."

Sing, Anna, Sing

Belinda Grimaudo Greyburn

This interview takes place over coffee at the kitchen table in my mother's home in Windsor, Ontario. My seventy-three-year-old mother, a resident of Canada since the mid-1960s, was born and raised in Sicily, Italy. I asked her to tell me stories from when she was a young girl.

~~~

"Let me tell you the story about the drunken pig," Mom says, getting up to bring me a homemade Sicilian cookie. "That one's funny."

"Yeah, but I don't get a chance to see you in that story, Mom. I want to hear about when you were little, in Italy. What was it like growing up there?"

"Sometimes, when you tell things about your family, honey, people don't understand. It was a different culture, a different time."

I give Mom a look to signify that I won't let her off that easily. Reluctantly, she takes a seat. She stirs her coffee, places the teaspoon on her napkin, and passes me the sugar.

"I was born in 1938, so I was still young during World War II. I lived with my parents, my sister Pina and my younger sister, Franca, who was severely disabled. At that time, whatever you produced, whether you had a farm or other type of industry, you had to relinquish it to the government and, in exchange, they would give you food stamps. The instituted rations were meagre, and if you had five people in your family, you had just enough bread for five people—no more, no less. You couldn't celebrate a religious holiday with a special meal because there was nothing extra. You had absolutely no money for anything.

"As the war progressed, it became increasingly difficult for many people to feed their families and survive. A black market began. Instead of handing everything over to the government, people would save a little here and hide a little there and either sell it themselves or give it to someone to sell for them on the black market.

"My father, a risk taker, bought from these people. In addition to what he held back on his own farm, he purchased beets, fava beans, wheat and other foods, and he would travel to other cities to sell them. These cities were on the other side of the mountain. To travel, my father either voyaged through the mountains or through seaside passages. We didn't have cars back then, only the traditional *carretto*—a colourful Sicilian-style carriage hooked to a mule."

"Why did he travel to these other cities?" I ask. "Couldn't he sell them in Alcamo?"

"Not every city grew the same types of crops. By selling in another city, my father could also purchase things that we didn't have.

"Travelling by mule and cart took several hours and was risky. By day, you took a chance with the police. If they stopped you, they could take everything you had. It happened to my father once. A blockade had been set up and the police were about to push back the hay in the cart and find the hidden goods. My father approached the police officer and said, 'I have family. Do you have family?' The police officer nodded.

"'Okay,' my father said. 'Tomorrow, come and find me at this address. I'll make sure your family gets fed.' The next day, the police officer showed up and my father gave him everything he could.

"After that, he travelled by night. To make it to the next city for the morning, he had to leave by three a.m. The route through the mountains could be dangerous. The path was dark. Only two oil lanterns hung on either side of the carriage. The cities below had their lights extinguished for fear of air raids. But my father had other worries beside the war and the dark—*ladri*. How do you say it?"

"Thieves," I say.

"Yes, thieves. Once, coming home from working on the farm, it rained and he placed his bread in the satchels of the mule's saddle. During the walk home, a thief snuck up on the other side of the mule, slit the satchel, and removed the bread without him knowing it. My father arrived home empty-handed. In the mountains, they were not so *gentili* (nice). We heard stories of thieves taking everything from travellers, including the mule and cart, leaving the victim on foot and alone in the mountains.

"They robbed because they had no food, no clothes, no home—nothing. They were desperate, but not evil. They had a code of honour, too. If they heard a family was passing through, they would not cause trouble. They had no intention of scaring children. They let peasants travelling from city to farm pass safely.

"In the summertime, when school was over, I would beg my father to take me with him. Sometimes he would say no, but other times, he would let me come along. I loved it."

"Were you ever scared?"

"For me, it was like a vacation! I saw the mountains and the sea, and when we reached the city, we stayed with friends and I explored the villages."

"How was travelling through the mountains?"

"I slept for most of the way. My father loaded the cart with beans and wheat and put hay on top for me to sleep on. From time to time, he woke me up and said in Sicilian, 'Sing, Anna, sing. Keep me company.'

"I sang all the time, at home and in church, so this was a pleasure for me. I had a beautiful, high voice, and I sang love songs in the darkness. You could hear my voice echo across the valleys. We were always safe, no one bothered us. We reached the city by the morning and sold all of our goods over two or three days. My father always made a point of buying a little gift for my mother before we returned. He adored her."

I smile at Mom.

"It was my choice to go. I loved being with my father and I loved travelling."

She gets up to stir the pasta sauce cooking on the stove.

"Let me tell you about the drunken pig," Mom says. "Now *that's* a funny story."

Ajarn

Anne Yendell

After our weekly session at the gym, I walk with my Muay Thai coach next door for morning coffee at Mimi's, a family-run café in midtown Toronto. Dan Caron and I became friends at the peak of his amateur boxing career, when he was northeastern Canada's welterweight low kick boxing champion. Now thirty-five, Dan has retired from the ring.

Dan's story is based on previous conversations and from a formal interview. I asked Dan to tell me about how he got his start in boxing, who influenced his career and his plans for the future on the other side of the ropes.

~~~

My cousin Rob was an amateur boxer in London, Ontario. His family spent holidays with mine in Welland. He was a lot older than me. My dad was a drunk, and I rarely saw him, even though he lived in town. When I was six years old, I followed Rob around and bugged him with lots of questions about training and competitions. My mom says that she'd sometimes catch me shadowboxing in the bathroom mirror. I was too young to take boxing lessons, so I was enrolled in karate when I was eight. Ever since I was little, my mom has taught me how to deal with obstacles. From what I'd seen, she'd done that her whole life. She grew up in St. Catharine's with a black father and a white mother. She knew discrimination and poverty.

Anyway, I was a small kid, and maybe she thought karate would be good for me. Turned out, I was a natural at martial arts.

In elementary school, I never got bullied or picked on, and I got into maybe two fights. I had a good mouth on me, and there were always others who would fight my fights. When you can defend yourself, you're probably not going to get bullied. You won't let somebody push you around or talk down to you 'cause you know you can beat 'em up. You don't get scared. Victims get scared, try to lash out—or worse, they withdraw.

So I kept up with the karate and, at thirteen, I added Japanese jujitsu to the mix. In jujitsu they taught me the grappling techniques for the ninety percent of fights that will eventually end up on the ground.

In high school I fell in with the wrong crowd. Most days I'd get high after school and get into some kind of trouble. At nineteen, I decided that it was time to turn myself around, to get myself back in shape and learn to box. By the time I'd finished high school, I was boxing competitively while making a living in construction.

In 2000 I moved to Toronto, and a few years later I met Jim Marinow. He probably had the biggest impact of anyone on my life. I had just finished a sparring session at Adrenaline when I caught Jim's Muay Thai class. I was like, "Full contact fighting is amazing! Check out those kicks, those knee, shin and elbow strikes and the punches!" I asked if I could train with him and right away, we hit it off. Ha! At the time I was like, What else would I rather do with the rest of my life? I knew I didn't want to go back to school, and I didn't want to stay working in construction. So for the next six years we worked, trained and coached together at Adrenaline, Atlas and at Sports Club. In 2009, Jim opened his own fight club, Hook Up

Muay Thai Boxing, where I continued to Thai-box while running their western-style boxing program.

Back when we first met, Jim was still in his early forties. He had a fifth-degree black belt in Goju-ryu karate and still competed at an international level. His dream was to attract and train athletes to compete at the national team level. His challenge was—and still is—to find the right fighters. Not those kids who grow up playing with action figures and watching UFC on TV, but real Muay Thai competitors. A guy can be a world-class athlete, the next big thing, but if he isn't a decent human being, doesn't demonstrate self-discipline, doesn't respect his teacher, his team, his club and his opponents, then Jim knows that he won't fit in at Hook Up. So, Jim won't train him. He follows the "old school" Thai tradition. He believes that to be successful, a fighter's Thai-boxing club must also become his family.

Over the past decade, Jim has taught me a hell of a lot about physical conditioning, mental preparation, commitment and coaching. For example, when I'm instructing a competitive fighter at Hook Up, we'll do a full round with a bag, and when it's over, we'll do a round of punishment, like power shots, twenty times. You've gotta get to the point where you're completely done, and then learn that you have it in you to drive yourself further. That's why a fight is the ultimate challenge. In a training situation you can ease up or even stop, but in a fight, you have no choice. You've got to push yourself even harder during that next round because it's your opponent's objective to hurt you, and he's waiting for you to fatigue and let down your guard. It's my job to prepare a fighter for that moment. As Jim would say, "Your fight brings you to the pinnacle of your training."

Jim also showed me how I could improve my performance and my focus with visualization exercises. On the night before a fight, we would do a mental rehearsal for the next day's competition. I'd imagine my walk-out, the lights, the sound of the crowd. I'd see myself moving toward the ring, feeling calm, greeting my opponent. I'd run through all the combinations and sequences of punches and kicks, until the final round, when I'd envision myself the winner. Because in boxing, you can't look around or get distracted by something unexpected, even for a second, or you'll get hit. But if you've done your mental run-through, you're prepared for anything. You won't be nervous. You won't worry about getting hurt. You can concentrate on the moment and you're free to think, I'm gonna be the first one to get in there, the first one to throw punches. I'm gonna keep coming at my opponent, and I won't stop until I win.

Jim was at his best when I was competing in the ring. My former boxing coach could get really negative during a fight. He'd say, "Caron, look alive. Don't let him see that he can rattle you...you gotta find a way in...what the hell are you doing out there?" That kinda talk.

When a coach tells you that you'd better hurry up and knock out your opponent, he could be pushing you just when you need to conserve energy. A fighter is already riled up, and he needs his mind put at ease. When I returned to my corner, Jim would tell me that I was doing great. He'd break things down, tell me what I needed to do, but in a positive way. Like maybe Jim just noticed that the other guy is dropping his left hand, and he'd remind me to throw more crosses. He might also change up the game plan a little. But somewhere in there, Jim would find a moment to remind me that this was what I'd trained for and what I'd dedicated years of my life to. Then he'd say, "So, Dan, this guy really wants to hurt you. What are you gonna do about it?" Ha!

Of course, I eventually paid a price for all those fights and for being a latecomer to the ring. In 2004, I damaged my right eye in an amateur fight when my opponent's thumb caught in the ridge of my helmet. Without the headgear, his hand probably would've slipped off. The hospital's ophthalmologists worried about long-term vision damage from the retinal tears and recommended that I stop fighting. I blamed it on the headgear.

Then in 2009, I was preparing for the first professional kickboxing fight of my career when I decided to take a pro boxing fight at Casino Rama. It'd been over a year since I'd western-style boxed. I had only a month to train. But the fight organizers were having a hard time finding an opponent for the Puerto Rican contender, and anyway, I figured I could use the experience at the professional level. Four thousand spectators looked on, and in a flash knockdown, my opponent won the fight. Man, I took a lot of ribbing at the gym after that. Ha! The Canadian Professional Boxing Federation suspended me for sixty days pending an MRI. I left that fight angry with my coaches for the match up and my lack of preparation, and more determined to focus on my Muay Thai training.

I realize now that thirty-one was probably too old to begin a career in pro boxing or pro fighting. Most fighters have reached their peak at that age or their skills are beginning to diminish. Now I'm on medication all the time, but the headaches still return whenever my heart rate elevates. Let's face it, if a stroke doesn't get you first, most fighters will wind up with "punch-drunk syndrome" or, ultimately, like Ali, with Parkinson's. No one wants to admit that there's a connection between hits to the head and headaches, impaired vision, speech, concentration and coordination, but my own experience tells me otherwise.

So, at Hook Up, we have a couple of guys coming up that are not bad. Jim is right. You need a ten-to-fifteen year sprint to build up a pro fighter. It's like what I saw last spring at the gyms in Thailand. The Thai master, or *Ajarn*, told me that he was just six years old when he moved into his club in Koh Phangan. Now at sixty, he has over four hundred fights under his belt. I'll never forget how he chain-smoked as he watched our Canadian team run the two-mile beach at Haad Rin at sunrise. How his joints must have ached from the years of wear and tear! He was one tough motherfucker.

While we would rest during the afternoon heat, my Ajarn would return to train the kids at the school. I once watched him teach them how to beat their shins and hands with bamboo sticks. It's called "cortical remodelling" and it builds up bone and kills nerve endings. Just like the Ajarn, those ten-to-twelve-year-old boys were mostly orphans, who had nowhere else to go but the clubs. They join, train and fight to make money to support themselves and their families. When they fight, it's mostly the gangsters who drive the betting system. It's rough. It's like human cockfighting.

So, for now, I teach and coach boxing and Muay Thai. I've begun to practise Brazilian jiu-jitsu—no strikes and no punches to the face. It's gonna be okay for me. Sometimes I think, What if I get thrown or hit in the head by accident? But, nah, that's probably not going to happen.

Martina V: Sex Worker

Joseph Dunlop

Martina, a twenty-seven-year-old sex worker, agrees to meet me at Tim Hortons on Queen Street in the Beaches. I identify Martina by her red baseball cap. She wears a hoodie, jeans and running shoes, and looks like a university student. Martina, five-foot-six with shoulder-length dirty blonde hair, is university-educated and articulate.

I ask only one question, "How did you become involved in sex work?"

Martina speaks nonstop for the next hour.

~~~

I was born and raised in Mississauga in a four-bedroom suburban home on a well-maintained cul-de-sac. My father was a Slovenian immigrant who, upon arriving in Toronto in 1974, lucked out finding a high-paying union job in the maintenance department of the Oakville Ford assembly plant. He resembled John Astin, the American actor who played Gomez Addams on *The Addams Family*. He had the same black moustache and receding hairline and was considered handsome.

My father was well-known for being helpful, generous and gifted at making Slovenian kielbasa. He soon became a prominent member of Mississauga's Slovenian Catholic community. One of his mentors, my godfather, Father Aloysius Ambrozic, became Archbishop of Toronto in 1990 and was a frequent guest in our home.

My father was thirty-eight years old when he met my twenty-year-old mother at Our Lady of the Miraculous Medal, a Slovenian church in Etobicoke. They married one year later and had three daughters in quick succession. I have a photo of my mom, my sisters and me, with our fine blonde hair blowing in the wind, in front of our house in 1986. My mom is beautiful in an Elisha Cuthbert way, but seems far too young to have a baby in a stroller as well as a two-year-old—me—by one hand and a three-year-old by the other.

People often joked that my father, as the only male in the house, was blessed to be surrounded by four beautiful women. Indeed, we appeared to be a happy, successful immigrant family—but it was a fiction, a public facade of perfection. Our private walls hid hurt, pain, anger and violence.

My father verbally and physically abused all of us, especially my mom. We never knew what triggered his outbursts. Whenever he arrived home and immediately began to close the windows, we knew to be afraid. He didn't want the neighbours to hear his forthcoming rampage.

He pushed my mother down the stairs more than once and frequently shoved her to the ground. My first broken bone occurred when I was about six. I tried to prevent my dad from jumping on my mom as she cowered on the floor. He picked me up and threw me on the kitchen table. Both the table and my ulna broke. He told the emergency room doctor I fell off the slide in the park.

Also, unknown to my mother, my father sexually abused my youngest sister and me. My first memory is of my dad guiding my hand along his hard penis as we watched TV. I can still feel the texture of the couch, and if I close my eyes, I can smell the strudel my mom was cooking upstairs in the kitchen. The sexual abuse ceased when I was seven and my sister was five. To this day, we don't know what triggered him to stop, but we were relieved when he did.

My father was very strict—typical of good, Slovenian dads. As teenagers, my sisters and I weren't allowed to go to parties, or to date. I had two very close girlfriends, but was forbidden to eat at their tables or sleep overnight in their homes. I quickly learned to be duplicitous as a survival technique. I claimed to join several clubs at school to explain why I came home so late, but the only thing I really joined was the after-school pot parties in my friend Sue's basement. I lost my virginity there, to a guy who I naively thought liked me.

U of T Mississauga was two kilometres from my family home, but I begged and pleaded to attend McMaster in Hamilton. I desperately wanted to escape my home life. My dad, of course, wanted to save money as well as keep me under his thumb. He would not relent. I was nineteen—there was grade thirteen in those days. Finally, with my mom's secret permission, I packed up and left one night when my dad wasn't home. A friend helped me move my stuff to Hamilton.

I had saved enough from a part-time job at the snack bar in the arena for tuition, but not enough for a year's living accommodations as well. With next to nothing to put down for first month's rent, I got a dive bachelor apartment in downtown Hamilton, complete with peeling paint, water damage, green mould and cockroaches. It stank, but worst of all, once October came, it was cold. I couldn't afford to pay my gas bill, and in my naivete, I hoped that the heat from the apartments on both sides would keep me warm. I was wrong. I could see my breath when I woke up in the morning. The water in the toilet had a thin layer of ice. My feet ached from the cold floor.

I kept warm at school all day. When I wasn't in my business classes, I studied or slept in the library. I packed peanut butter sandwich lunches from ingredients I picked up at the food bank. In the evening, I took a part-time job at a bar twelve blocks from my horrible apartment.

I chose to apply at that particular bar because it had a richer clientele than the bars in my own neighbourhood. It was a warm, friendly place, a lot like the bar in *How I Met Your Mother*. I quickly learned, as all waitresses do, that wearing short skirts, showing cleavage and flirting outrageously paid off in bigger tips. I dreaded closing when I knew I had to return to my freezing apartment. The first time a guy asked me back to his place, I didn't hesitate to say yes. I knew I'd be warm at least for the next eight hours. Funny, huh? The first time I prostituted myself wasn't for money; it was for heat.

As a business major, I quickly realized that I could sell myself for a lot more than a little warmth. I wanted to know about the sex trade, so I pretended to be doing a paper on prostitution and started asking questions of patrons in the bar. I was doing some research, did they know any escorts? Did they know how I could contact one? Eventually, a guy knew a guy who had a cousin who knew a friend who had a phone number. I called and told the woman who answered the phone, Lisa, the truth: I was considering becoming an escort. She met with me and offered me a working room in the four-bedroom apartment that served as the home base for her escort service. The cost was twelve hundred dollars a month. Her job was to screen clients and ensure there was always someone—her or her sister—in the front room in case of trouble.

The twelve hundred dollars concerned me—I didn't have anywhere near that kind of money—but she assured me I would make that amount in one weekend. The men who phoned her service were middle-aged, usually divorced, and fairly wealthy. They were willing to pay three hundred dollars a visit.

Thus began a very successful partnership between me and Lisa. In my four years of university, I netted one hundred and forty thousand dollars. After paying tuition, renting a beautiful new apartment, buying a car and paying living expenses, I had forty thousand dollars in savings when I graduated in 2006. Not bad. I was better off than my classmates, many of whom were thousands of dollars in debt.

I moved to Toronto to start a business career on Bay Street. I thought my escort days were behind me. Within three months, I landed a junior position at a global investment firm. I worked fourteen-hour days and was happy to do it. Unfortunately, as one of the least senior people, I was laid off during the financial crisis eighteen months later. I allowed myself exactly one year to look for other work before I went back to escorting. I've been at it ever since.

My plan now is to work as an escort until I have enough money to start my own legitimate business. Escorting is a very profitable way to make a living, but it's not a long-term career.

My body is my business. Whenever someone who doesn't know me asks me what kind of business I'm in, I just answer, "I'm in human relations."

Molecular Templates

Shaan Gupta

I walk up to the Master of Biotechnology office at the University of Toronto Mississauga. The nameplate on the door reads, "Leigh Revers, Associate Director of MBiotech." I hold two medium double-doubles. I knock lightly, taking care not to spill the coffee.

"Hey! So sorry I'm late. I was caught up in a meeting," says Dr. Revers in a British accent as he walks up from behind me. "Is that coffee for me?"

"Yup."

"Great! That's the perfect way to start a meeting!"

Dr. Revers ushers me into a meeting room. We sit across from each other at a large glass boardroom table. On one wall hangs a whiteboard with the words, "Net Present Value: The Time Value of Money," written in red marker and followed by a mathematical formula. To the left of the whiteboard sit two iMacs and a big LCD flat screen mounted to the wall.

"What would you like to interview me about, Shaan?" Dr. Revers asks.

"I was hoping you could tell me about that biotech company you created and sold for five million dollars before you started teaching here at UTM."

"Everyone wants to hear that story!"

"Why don't we start with you telling me about the drug you developed?"

"We started studying this molecule called Shiga-like toxin from bacteria that makes you sick. These bacteria cause hamburger disease. You know, when Jack in the Box had those outbreaks of E. coli poisoning? Those E. coli are normally quite friendly and you have them in your gut all the time, but these particular E. coli strains have a bunch of extra genes that make them rather nasty, and one of those encodes a nasty protein that's really toxic. It's as toxic as ricin, one of the most poisonous substances out there, so it kills cells really well.

"The idea was, if this stuff can kill cells maybe we can tailor it to kill the cells we want it to kill. So the question was, What kind of cells would you want to kill? Cancer cells! So we worked with this bacterium that kills cells and made it selective for cancer cells."

"What happened next?"

"We developed the idea and tried to shop it around and everyone really liked it. Then we went around and raised capital from venture capitalists—people who take risks by investing in new ideas. We visited anonymous offices for a number of months and went up glass elevators into tall buildings and into indistinguishable conference rooms to meet people who would be interested in our technology, or not. We managed to corral a group of people who were interested. They gave us half a million dollars in cash, enabling us to start a company. So we created Molecular Templates.

"I had a piece of the ownership. It was very exciting. For seven years, we were set up in a laboratory no bigger than this room; it couldn't have been bigger than four hundred square feet. We were working inside a hospital on a deadly toxin.

"One day we realized that maybe our technology wouldn't work. You have to recognize that 299 of every 300 drugs that go into clinical trials fail, and we weren't even in clinical trials yet, so it was very likely that we were going to fail. It's like playing the lottery, really. But I think entrepreneurship is about being prepared to fail. You know—throwing yourself at a brick wall until one day you smash through it, hopefully.

"Now we get to the more interesting part of the story—when we started to run out of money. The Canadian funds began to siphon away. We'd spent it all. We knew that everybody was going to be out of a job. It was really quite a scary time because you've worked with these people for seven years.

"It was a sad day when in February 2007 the company closed its doors.

"I came to work here at the university after that, and left that life behind…at least I thought I did. But naturally, you can't really leave those things behind. They're a part of you, and as a founder, that's particularly difficult to let go—it's like having a child.

"I went around giving presentations to try and find investors, and by chance, I was introduced to Stephanie De Grandis. Stephanie is the woman who cloned the gene for Shiga-like toxin, the molecule I'd been working on for the previous seven years. She was excited when she learned about what I had been doing. She said she didn't want the project to die and she'd help introduce me to whomever she could who might express an interest.

"I was lucky enough to be introduced to some American investors who came up from Pittsburgh. Stephanie had organized this showcase and invited me to present. I gave my presentation and it was pretty gloomy, to be honest. But Stephanie came to me after lunch and said they really liked it. We discussed it more over dinner and they invited me down to Pittsburgh. They introduced me to their specialist in oncology, Frank Zafferstein. He looked at it and he really liked it.

"We spent most of the summer putting another presentation together. We went back down there for the final presentation, which happened to be the day when US Treasury bills went through the floor—Black Monday. We were going to seal that deal for, like, three million bucks US, and they literally, that day, pulled the rug out from under us. They said, 'We are hemorrhaging cash. We can't give you any capital. We can't make any more investments because the whole financial community is grinding to a halt as we speak.'

"They make decisions that fast. When we flew back, we felt pretty depressed.

"I got a phone call a week afterwards from my partner, Eric Palmer. He said, 'You know what? I still think we have a chance. I still believe in this technology. I have a friend down in Texas and he expressed an interest. Let's try that.'

"So we started all over again. This time we had to go to Austin, Texas, to meet these people with big ten-gallon hats and shoestring ties. They really liked the technology and they really liked Eric as well. I don't know what they thought about me.

"We went through the process again and this time they set a date to close in the spring of 2009. I flew down and went to the hotel. We cracked some champagne. They actually signed. We had a slap-up meal. They ordered cake bread and a fantastic California red wine, among the greatest red wines I've ever drunk.

"They raised two and a half million dollars US, which was put into the company, and they reinvented it as Molecular Templates US, based outside of Austin, Texas, in a place called Georgetown. That's where it is now.

"I could never have predicted that sequence of events. By luck I was introduced to each of these people. There's no way that chain of events could have ever been predicted, and yet it led to success."

"So is Molecular Templates still open?" I ask.

"It is. In fact, the news is good. Molecules that they've developed are about to enter into clinical trials."

"Are they still working on the Shiga-like toxin?"

"They are. It's still based on the Shiga-like toxin, the candidate molecule I found in 2004 in Canada.

"You could argue the only success is to find a drug that cures cancer. But no drug cures cancer. So, at what point do you measure success? I'm going to sit back and say if the molecule I discovered ends up in a patient, then that is a major success. Even if it doesn't work, that is a huge leap. Now, who knows? It might even show some benefit in the patient. That's even more exciting."

"So, when in this process did you get your Aston Martin?"

"That's a very good sort of endnote to the whole thing. I turned forty in 2010. When I turned forty, I decided I really wanted to do some of the things that had been burning in me. The Aston Martin was something I could predict, unlike all the other stuff that happened to me that I couldn't."

Eva Wilkens

Sara Middleton

This story is based on an interview with my grandmother, Eva Wilkens. She talks about her experiences in Germany during the Second World War. It's written from her perspective.

~~~

I grew up in Gross-Jestin in Pomerania, Germany. It was a small town with less than a thousand people. But it was beautiful. We lived two kilometres from the Baltic Sea. Every day me and my older brother, Johannes, would cut through the Hindenburg's property, over the meadows, and go swimming in the sea. The white sand stretched for miles.

It was a good life. We never wanted for anything; our bellies were always full. Gross-Jestin had a school, two churches, two stores, a bakery, a drug store—everything we needed.

My family was well off, not in money, but in property. We had the biggest apple orchard for miles and miles. I remember taking a walk with Hindenburg's granddaughter one day and she admitted to me that she and her sister would steal our apples when we had our backs turned. My mother, Mutti, always told us to keep an eye out.

Paul Von Hindenburg was the President of Germany for a time. He was in opposition to Hitler, and a friend to my father, until Hindenburg died in 1934.

The name "Hitler" wasn't mentioned a lot. If it was, I didn't pay attention to it. I just assumed he was a good guy. I was young. One Christmas, when I was about ten, I thought it would be a good idea to give my papa a picture of Hitler. When Papa opened my gift, he looked at me and calmly said, "Thank you." He beckoned for me to follow him. I followed Papa into his bedroom. My father placed his finger over his lips. He opened the bottom drawer of his dresser and put the picture of Hitler face down in the drawer and covered it. Papa shook his head once and never again took the picture out. Not a word was said, in case there were listening ears.

Before the war started, my parents never told me to salute Hitler. So, I never raised my arm when everyone else saluted—until they made us.

Germany went to war when I was thirteen.

Not everyone in Gross-Jestin opposed Hitler. My father's sister and her husband, the Wegners, were Nazis. Wegner was always jealous of my father because he had a bigger home and a better life. But that's just the way it was. When the draft began, my father was supposed to be safe because he was too old and he was sick. But Wegner, and the mayor of our town…those Nazis…they were supposed to be drafted, but because of their connections, they were able to weasel their way out of it. They pointed their fingers at Papa instead. Wegner and the mayor remained safe, and my sick father was taken to fight a war he didn't believe in.

In the following years, we were able to remain in our home. But there was no school or church. Our days were spent trying to stay safe. Our town eventually became the frontline between the Russians and the Germans. The Germans didn't realize civilians were still there. Every night we heard gunfire and cannons. There would be a bang, and then light, and then a bang, and then light. Like fireworks. I remember the first time I heard real fireworks, years later in Hamburg. I was so startled; they sounded exactly like the explosions during the war.

One night, my family was huddled in our damp basement on a sack of potatoes. The house shook every few minutes from the cannons and gunfire. We survived the night, and in the morning, Mutti took us to the neighbour's house. She figured we would be safer in numbers. I remember walking across the meadow. I felt a strong urge to put my back down. As I hit the ground, a bullet flew over my head. I could hear the whistling. I think God saved me that day. I don't know why.

One day when the fighting was bad, the Russians told us to leave and find a safe place. We were sent east where the fighting used to be. We stayed with some soldiers. They fed us and they were very nice. We went back and forth between there and home for a time. At home, many of the women and children in town moved into our house for safety. There were about twenty-five children and ten women. We were all scared. Two of my friends were poisoned by their grandmother because she felt death was better than this life.

The soldiers liked to play games with us. One day the Russians told all the males, my brother Johannes included, to go to the market-place. I didn't want him to go. He never returned home.

Then, on March 6, 1945, the Russians came into our town. They told us to pack our things and leave; Gross-Jestin was now Russian territory.

Many died that day. My Russian nanny begged for her life. But they raped and killed her in our home. The soldiers let me say good-bye to her dead body.

We took only what we could carry—food and one blanket each. Our party consisted of me, my mother, my aunt, my little sister Ruth and my little brother Ernie. We were headed west, to my mother's old town where her parents still lived. We walked and walked and walked. It felt endless. We slept outside, we slept in a train station, we slept on grass, we slept on tables, we slept in a school, we slept on benches. We never complained. At the end of the day, we were too tired to care where we slept.

Wherever we went, we had to beg for food. Many of the places that we passed through lay empty. All the homes had been abandoned. Sometimes we would find an apple tree and we would eat the apples. It reminded me of home. We wouldn't have eaten them, though, if we thought it was stealing.

We walked for a few weeks. One day a train passed us and Mutti told us to jump on. We were so exhausted and the idea of not having to walk was wonderful. So, we jumped on. We thought the train was headed west, but it took us south. We went many miles out of our way.

After almost a month of walking, we made it to the border of the Russian and British zones in central Germany—no-man's-land. There were guards everywhere. Each night I could hear people being shot—by the Russians or the British, I don't know—for trying to cross. We waited for over a month, trying to find a way to cross. Finally, we met a farmer who had property rights on no-man's-land, who was allowed to cross freely. After many arrangements, he agreed to take us across, hidden in his hay wagon. He risked his life for my family.

My mother was scared. If we were found, we would all be killed. I volunteered to go first. I went with my brother Ernie, who was five at the time. We hid in the back of the hay wagon. Halfway through no-man's-land, we transferred to another farmer's wagon, who took us to the other side. There was no time to feel scared.

After we made it across, I took Ernie's hand and we knocked on doors to find a place to sleep. I didn't worry for my family. Worrying made you do nothing, and I couldn't afford to do nothing. We found a place to stay and in the morning the family made us breakfast. Then Ernie and I went to the border where the British were. There was Mutti, walking towards us, safe and unharmed.

After a couple more weeks of walking, we made it to my grandparents' house. Our journey was finally over. When I knocked on the door, there was Johannes. I threw myself at him and hugged him as tightly as I could. We both thought the other was dead. Johannes told us he ran away. He made his own way across Germany and had arrived at our grandparents' house only a month before us.

The war ended a couple months later. It wasn't until 1947 that we found out what happened to my father. We made contact with a German-speaking pastor in France who knew my father. Papa was put in an American-French prisoner-of-war camp in France. He eventually died of starvation. But those kinds of things happened. You had to live through it.

We never made it back to Gross-Jestin, to the sea or to the white sands. We had everything we wanted there…at least for a short time.

Interview with Tevyah

Jason Swetnam

Tevyah Lytle, my wife's youngest brother, has four siblings: my wife Della, Meda, Millie and Solomon. Their dad, Bob, and his wife, Brenda, followed a religious movement called The Message until Bob died. Believers follow the teachings of Brother Joseph Branham. Most people would consider The Message to be a cult. Recorded sermons of Brother Branham blared in the background of the Lytle house—and so did Bob.

Every member of the Lytle family carries around their own particular brand of damage caused by Bob and his angry, dogmatic, religious ways.

Tevyah is a roofer. He spent a week at my house in March in transition from living in Vancouver to resettling in Pittsburgh. Tevyah told me that he needed to leave Vancouver because he wanted to start over. He had a drug problem and a troubled relationship.

When I think of Tevyah, I picture his stuff piled around the couch that he slept on in my living room—a laptop with skateboard and metal band stickers, a well-used skateboard, a leather jacket poking out from under a cut-off jean jacket with a Slayer patch across the back that matched the red Slayer tattoo across his wrist, and the black toque he tucked his long hair under every day.

I'd see multiple bottles or cans of beer scattered on the coffee table and kitchen counter when I got up at six-thirty to get ready for work.

My brother-in-law stayed with us for a week. Then I drove him to Beaver, where his mom lives, just outside of Pittsburgh. I stayed for the night. Tevyah and I went out for a few pints to do this interview.

Over the years, Tevyah has surprised me with his insight into himself, his siblings, and his parents. He shares this insight in the candid telling of his story.

We order two pints and I ask him about his childhood.

~~~

I remember Dad being a jerk, always yelling. I didn't like it when he was around. He was just always yelling about everything, at Mom, at me. He yelled at me a lot. He compared me to Solomon, my older brother, a lot. When Dad was around, there was a lot of yelling and religion. Solomon turned to it when he was in his early twenties, looking for some guidance or something. Dad kind of moulded him around it. I didn't like it at all. It was force-fed.

I was told that Dad had a revelation when he was in Jeffersonville, Indiana. He was walking over a bridge and this desire led him into this church, and that's what he based the rest of his life on.

I was told he was sick. I remember him taking pills, but I didn't find out until later that it was for schizophrenia. After a while he convinced himself, or someone did, that he didn't need to take them, so he stopped. With that kind of sickness, you can convince yourself that you don't need them. I was told in my teens that my dad was sick, but I think it was an excuse.

Dad never worked. He just blamed everyone else for his problems.

I first stuck up for myself when I was living with them at Jean's, a motel outside of Pittsburgh. It was the middle of the winter and the car door froze. He started freaking out, screaming and yelling at

Mom and me because the door wouldn't close. The latch was frozen, so I fixed it. I wiggled it around and I fixed it. I closed the door and I told him, "Shut the fuck up, it's not a big deal, you're yelling about nothing," and he shut up! It was the first time that I told him to shut up and he did!

When I was a kid, I was totally scared of him. I hated him. I remember one day—I must have been ten—I was walking up the street with him after we left the house. We lived in Middle Sackville. He belted me right on the side of the road. Smacked me right in the face. I don't remember why; I did something and he didn't like it. He hit me right on the street. He said to me that day that he would never hit me again. But he kicked the shit out of me a couple of times after that. I remember.

He kicked the shit out of me when I stole money from Austin Amos Stewart's house. I stole thirty dollars and got caught. He made me bleed that day when he found out. I was thirteen. He punched me in the mouth—I was bleeding—and that was one of the worst days that I got it from him, except for the day when he told me that I was....

I didn't want to go to school. So he came up and he grabbed me out of bed. He grabbed my leg and pulled me out right onto the floor. He said, "Get the fuck up!" My mom couldn't get me out of bed because I hated school. I was in grade six. He pulled me out of that bed and I hit the floor. I got up and I started getting ready. I came downstairs and he was yelling at me. He was saying I was a mistake and all the usual things that he always said to me.

I hated him. I fucking hated him. He was not nice to me. He wasn't nice in general but he was really not nice to me. Everyone has a bad taste in their mouth when it comes to Dad.

I got it pretty bad. Sol got it pretty bad, too.

He told me I was a mistake. So I told him he wasn't my father. He said, "You want me to take down my pants and show you where you came from?" I ran and he chased me. I made it to the kitchen door. He belted me pretty good. I got to the porch and he just laid into me. I had welts all over my back.

I went to a foster home for six months. I was twelve, in grade six. They foster parented another boy my age. He ended up killing himself. I lived there for six months. Dad didn't want me to. He took my hockey gear away. He didn't want me to play hockey because my coach was my therapist's husband, and he didn't like my therapist.

The therapy was about Alvin, my mother's brother, and all the shit that happened to me when I was eight. It came out when I was ten. I was in grade three. I didn't say anything until I was ten. I think it happened to me twice, and I didn't like it. I didn't like it and I did something about it.

I didn't allow it to happen again.

I refused to be in the same room as Alvin. When it happened the first time, it was kind of like a dream, like a bad dream, then it happened again, and I got myself out of the situation.

I remember it very vividly. I was eight years old. I was sleeping in the same bed as him. I was up against the wall. I had my back towards him, facing the wall. I had a blue onesie on with the zipper down the middle. I remember him putting me on top of him, back to chest, pulling down my zipper, fondling me. I remember his erection against my ass. I reached down to the side of the bed and I pulled myself off. Solomon was sleeping on the floor. I went out and got into bed with Mom and refused to ever be in the same room as him at night. They said, "Do you want to sleep with

Alvin?" I said, "No, I don't." I made a big stink about it. That was the second and last time.

Art, my mother's father, said to my dad, after everything came out, "Do you think that Tevyah is the only one that this happened to in this family?"

That meant I was not the only one who was molested in my family. He knew, they knew, and they didn't do anything about it. Where did Alvin learn this from? Someone did it to him, whether it was his dad or his brother, but it's in the family. It's all on my mom's side of the family. Alvin looks like a pedophile.

Denial is powerful. Solomon tried to tell Mom. He didn't come outright like I did. He tried to tell her something was wrong, and she didn't see the signs and she denied.

I told Dad and things started to happen.

It made me confused about my relationship with my dad because he treated me so bad, and when he did nice things for me, it made me confused.

I didn't believe Dad was sick. He was emotionally a baby, if anything, from being rejected when people were supposed to take care of him as a child. He didn't have the balls to fucking help himself. He just blamed. He took all his frustration and anger out on the people who loved him, and did till the very end, man, the very fucking end, kicking and screaming like a baby.

When Dad got sick, Solomon came home to help. Mom was here. He couldn't even wipe his own ass and he was fucking screaming at them. None of it even mattered to him. He was a fucking prick. I didn't like him and I told him that. The last day I saw him alive I said, "I don't like you." No, I said, "I love you Dad, but I don't like you."

He didn't say anything to me. He said things to Mom, and then Mom said them to me. He doesn't have balls. He never had balls. He is a bully, and that's what he taught me, how to be a bully.

The last day that I saw him alive summed up my whole fucking relationship with him—everything. It was the most horrible day I ever had with him. Everything I knew of him was there that day. I told him I didn't like him and he said to me all those fucking things he always said. "You're a mistake," "Your mother should have had an abortion," and "How dare you talk to me that way, you're going to burn in hell."

I said to him: "You're a sixty-seven-year-old man, and that's what you have to say to your son? That's what you have to say?"

My father made my life difficult. A man who has a child should do everything in his power to teach his son how to succeed, how to be a good man, and he didn't do that. Since Dad died, I got worse. I have a very bad temper. I started having panic attacks because I can't deal with emotions. I don't know how to express myself other than through anger. It's the only emotion that I have. I lost my fiancé because of it.

I stopped being able to deal with and keep my anger in check. I am always mad, over little things, things that Dad would get mad at. I am sitting in my house and I look on the floor. There is a piece of garbage on the floor and instead of getting up and picking it up and putting it in the garbage, I scream and yell about it, just like my dad.

85715753R00188

Made in the USA
Columbia, SC
04 January 2018